Making and Managing a

Smallholding

MICHAEL ALLABY

David & Charles
Newton Abbot   London   North Pomfret (Vt)

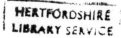
British Library Cataloguing in Publication Data
Allaby, Michael
Making and managing a smallholding.
1. Agriculture – Great Britain
2. Farms, Small – Great Britain
I. Title
631   S513.2
ISBN 0–7153–7803–1

Typeset by Trade Linotype Limited, Birmingham
and printed in Great Britain
by A. Wheaton & Co. Limited   Exeter
for David & Charles (Publishers) Limited
Brunel House   Newton Abbot   Devon

Published in the United States of America
by David & Charles Inc
North Pomfret Vermont 05053 USA

Contents

Introduction

Most of us are country people at heart. It is true that most of us were born and bred in large cities, but we need not delve very deep into our past to find rural ancestors. Scratch away the superficial layer of urban sophistication and inside us there is a country squire, a yeoman farmer, a wily peasant or a poacher, yearning for liberation.

The trouble is that most of us are tied to a daily routine that makes a rural life seem very remote; and when we glance wistfully at the property advertisements we see that the rural acres appeal to others as well as ourselves and that most of the others have more money than we have.

Yet there are degrees of possibility. In West Germany, many people have a very high standard of living based on a kind of urban–rural mix of lifestyles. They work part of the day in factories, offices or shops, and in the mornings and evenings, at weekends and in the holidays, they manage a few acres of land. This small-scale farming does not bring an income large enough to keep them, but it does much more than pay for itself. If it is 'hobby farming' it is comparatively profitable as the earnings derived from it are added to an ordinary wage. A survey of these part-time farmers conducted late in 1978 showed that their agricultural earnings amounted to more than 40 per cent of their wages from other sources. If you calculate 40 per cent of your own salary or wage and add that to your income as your farming profit, the attraction becomes obvious. Part-time farming is increasing in Britain, too. So it should, for agricultural land in Germany costs about two and a half times what it costs in this country, when allowance has been made for different costs of living.

While I hope this book may suggest ideas and enterprises to the part-time farmer, it is directed rather more at the person who wishes to work the land full-time, but on a small scale. It is a book of ideas, of problems and ways they may be overcome, and of general principles. It does not pretend to be a textbook of farming. There are such textbooks, but the only satisfactory way to learn how to farm is *to farm*, preferably on someone else's land or at a recognised college or other institution.

Much of this book is devoted to explaining how agriculture works in Britain—not in the sense of describing how plants are persuaded to grow or how cows are milked—but how the Government and the EEC affect farming, what land, buildings and equipment are needed to embark on particular enterprises, and sometimes an idea of what these cost, and how food is marketed. It is important to understand such matters if you are to enter the industry at any level. It is easier to run foul of the law than you may imagine.

I have tried to outline the most common types of farming and to show how climatic, topographical and economic constraints have led to their concentration in particular areas. From a brief glance at the geography of farming it is possible to see why land is graded as 'good' or 'bad' and why it is not a good idea to grow crops outside their geographic range. At this point, I have tried to give a little guidance in the search for a holding.

Land, buildings, equipment, stock and seed are expensive, although if you have paid off a mortgage on a town house, say, or have acquired a modest capital sum in some other way, the degree of achievement becomes that much more possible. I have outlined some of the ways in which capital may be raised, and I have explained farm tenancies and crofting, an ancient system of land tenure still practised in parts of Scotland and the northern islands. Once the holding has been acquired you will need to plan your farming regime. At this point you will encounter the Government, so I have tried to show how the farm support system works and where to obtain advice.

This takes us on to farming itself; I have described the general principles of the most important enterprises. Since many of these are profitable only when managed on a medium or large scale, I have tried to find ways in which they can be used to supply specialist markets with suggestions for more unusual enterprises

6

that might well collapse in confusion if they were attempted on anything but a small scale. Might it be possible to grow rye for its straw, which is excellent thatching material? Could you grow willow for basket making? Could you farm fish? Could you open a silk farm? You will find details of more conventional marketing methods, including all the statutory boards with which you must register if you plan to operate certain enterprises commercially, and I have explored less usual and perhaps more profitable ways to dispose of produce.

Finally we return to the position from which we began—that of outsiders—people to whom the countryside exists for purposes in addition to the production of commodities for profit. Farmers have thought too little about conservation, about the preservation of landscapes that are aesthetically pleasing, and all too often they have little consideration for the right of others to enjoy and experience the countryside. It is very easy to become obsessed with the efficiency and profitability of any business—and farming is no exception. In the end, we must remember that there is a real and important sense in which land cannot be owned by any individual. The countryside of Britain is not the private property of a small number of landowners who are entitled to exclude others from their domain. The countryside belongs to all of us. We have a right to enjoy it and a responsibility to treat it with respect.

If this book helps you unravel some of the complexities of farming, if it sparks off in you ideas that begin to make feasible a dream that seemed beyond the realms of possibility, then it will have succeeded.

As an aid I have used Imperial measures throughout the book. They are antiquated, obsolete even, and when you begin farming you will have to learn to use litres, kilograms, tonnes and hectares. For the moment, though, and for most of us, gallons, pounds, tons and acres seem more friendly.

1 The geography of it all

What grows where

In theory, you can grow any kind of crop anywhere. You could grow bananas at the North Pole if you were really determined. You would need to import soil, to erect large buildings with adequate heating, lighting, ventilation and irrigation systems, but it could be done. It sounds, and is, absurd, but it illustrates what is technologically feasible and it implies that constraints can be overcome and the range of farm enterprises that tradition associates with a particular area can be extended.

The practical limitations are economic. The reason no one moves up to the North Pole (where land is cheap) to open a banana plantation is that although it could be done, the cost of doing it would ensure that the bananas would be a great deal more expensive than those grown in the tropics. If there were more people living at the North Pole, all of whom were rather wealthy and hopelessly addicted to bananas, then the enterprise might be feasible if the additional production cost were less than the cost of transporting bananas from the tropics. As it is, the Arctic bananas would have to be sold in Europe and America, where they would be more expensive than tropical bananas—and the enterprise would fail.

Believe it or not, there is a lesson to be learned from this silly example, and that is that many generations of farmers have learned to survive economically by developing farming enterprises and methods that are appropriate for the conditions in which they are practised. It is sensible, then, to look at the farming that is most common in the area where you plan to settle. Tradition should not necessarily be allowed the final word; but if you depart from tradition you should do so deliberately, for a good reason, and with solutions ready for the problems you know you must face.

You do not need to visit every part of Britain to discover the types of farming and the way they are distributed, because overall a pattern exists that is fairly simple. Draw a line passing just to the west of Newcastle-upon-Tyne, then just to the east of Leeds, Sheffield and Coventry and south to Southampton. England and Wales to the west of that line are devoted mainly to livestock enterprises, and the land to the east is predominantly arable. The pattern continues into Scotland—the arable farms lying to the east and the stock farms to the west.

Most of the area devoted to livestock is engaged in dairying, with beef cattle and sheep being confined to the poorer, more hilly areas, where the pastures are less nutritious. The big cereal farms are located in Humberside, eastern Lincolnshire, down through Nottinghamshire, Leicestershire and Northamptonshire, across Cambridgeshire, Suffolk and into Norfolk, and to the south of the Midlands conurbation, where they merge into mixed farming and on into the mainly dairying regions. There are large cereal farms in Scotland, too, mainly in the south-east. Further north, wheat will not ripen; and in the Highlands neither soil nor climate are suitable for cereals.

There is a reason for the pattern. In the west of Britain the rocks are younger than those in the east. They are less weathered, they lie closer to the surface and in some moorland areas and in the mountains they crop out at the surface. So, generally, the western side of the country is more hilly, soils are usually thinner, and in some places they are extremely thin. In the east, the older, more weathered rocks are buried deep beneath soils of various kinds. The topography is gentler, the hills smaller and less steep, and in places the landscape is quite flat. It is easier to use the large fields that are more suited to crop growing in the east for that purpose; while western lowland fields are smaller and can contain livestock; again, the uplands are often unenclosed to provide stock, most commonly sheep, with the large areas they need to obtain an adequate diet from the poor pastures.

The topography also affects the climate. The eastern counties are low lying, which can give them very warm days in summer and autumn in places that are sheltered from the wind. This is important

9

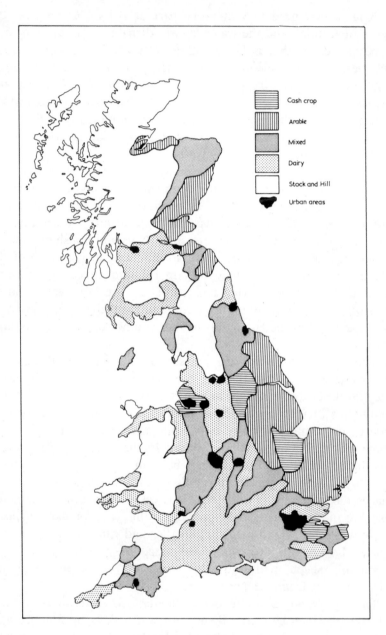

Types of farming in Britain

10

for ripening and drying grains. The east is also drier because weather moving to Britain from the west, which most of our weather does, brings moist air from the Atlantic which loses its moisture as it is forced to rise over the hills. So rainfall is higher in the west than in the east and this high rainfall is also a limiting factor to cereal production. In Cornwall and Devon, for example, where average summer and winter temperatures are higher than in most other parts of Britain, it is difficult to ripen grain. Some barley is grown and a little oats—all for feeding stock—but not much wheat.

Warm weather and a high rainfall favour grass and the western regions grow excellent pastures.

Although climate imposes restrictions on the kind of farming that is most practicable, there is no part of lowland Britain where climate alone precludes any kind of farming. Caithness supports prosperous stock farms and the Orkney Islands support beef and sheep, with some dairying. In Shetland, conditions are more difficult, partly because of the severity of the climate (especially the high winds) but mainly because of the rugged nature of the terrain and the poor, thin soils.

Land classification

Agricultural land is classified by the Department of Agriculture into five grades and these grades are used sometimes in describing land. The system of classification is reasonable, but the picture that emerges from it can be misleading; and farmers who manage to farm the poorer lands well and productively, often object to it. According to the official figures, less than three per cent of the farmland in England and Wales is Grade 1 and almost 40 per cent is Grade 3. This picture, which is derived from a survey that took seven years to complete, seems to contradict the impressions given by a tour of Britain, much of it past field after field of strong, healthy crops. No doubt William Cobbett would denounce the classification system as the product of corrupt urban minds, and many farmers would agree with him. Yet the system remains and while it may well contain errors with regard to individual small

11

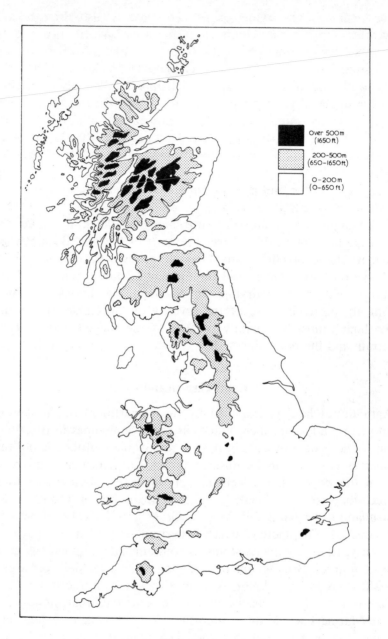

Over 500m
(1650 ft)

200-500m
(650-1650ft)

0-200m
(0-650 ft)

Topography

12

areas, in general it is useful. This is especially true for anyone contemplating the purchase of land and who has the entire country from which to choose a location.

Grade 1 land is defined as land with no physical limitations, or only very minor ones, to its agricultural use. Yields from it are consistently high and cropping can be extremely flexible because most crops, including the most exacting horticultural crops, can be grown on it.

Grade 2 land has some minor physical limitation that excludes it from Grade 1. There may be some restriction in the horticultural and arable root crops that can be grown; however, the range of possible enterprises is still wide.

Grade 3 land is more limited, due to the soil, relief, climate or some combination of these, and so the range of practicable enterprises is more restricted. Less-demanding horticultural crops can be grown, but on poorer Grade 3 land, root crops may only be suitable for forage crops. The main crops on Grade 3 land are likely to be cereals or grass, again depending on the climate.

Grade 4 land is quite severely restricted because of soil, relief, climate or some combination of them. Much Grade 4 land is under grass, with occasional fields of barley, oats or forage crops—all used to feed livestock.

Grade 5 land is severely limiting. Generally, it grows only grass, which may be no more than rough grazing, although occasionally pioneer forage crops are to be found. Rather more than 10 per cent of the farmland of England and Wales is classified as Grade 5 land, and the figure for Scotland is somewhat higher.

Land grades are not mentioned in property advertisements, which usually state no more than the current enterprise on the land (eg, dairy, stock, arable, etc). This is some guide, but you cannot rely entirely on the rather simplistic economic theory of comparative advantage. If you could, it would follow that the present farmer uses the land in the most profitable way possible; so that if the advertisement says 'stock', the land sounds like Grade 3, and possibly poor Grade 3 at that. However, the present occupier may be a bad farmer who does not know that his land is capable of more. He may not possess the capital that would have to be

13

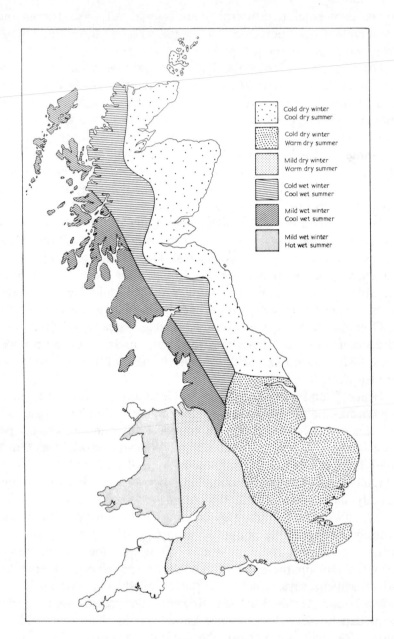

	Cold dry winter Cool dry summer
	Cold dry winter Warm dry summer
	Mild dry winter Warm dry summer
	Cold wet winter Cool wet summer
	Mild wet winter Cool wet summer
	Mild wet winter Hot wet summer

Climate

14

invested if the farm were to be upgraded. He may be bound by tradition, using the land in the way his father and grandfather did; and thus lack the imagination to see the potential of his farm as an outsider might see it, or not possess the courage to make fundamental changes. He may farm the way he does because he prefers his own methods. Despite all talk of economic pressures to which farmers are subjected, it remains a fact that many specialise in those enterprises they enjoy most. There is nothing wrong with this, of course, from the human point of view. The person who can grow magnificent vegetables may have no talent for livestock husbandry and the good dairy farmer might fail dismally with sheep.

It is possible to discover the land grade quickly because the whole of England and Wales have been mapped and these maps can be bought. Provided you know the location of the farm in which you are interested, you can buy the relevant sheet, which is based on the one-inch Ordnance Survey Map (7th series). The map costs £1.12 or, for some sheets, £4.33, plus postage and packing for one map 39p, for up to four maps 58p, or for five maps 73p. There is a report, costing 70p or 75p depending on the region, plus 9p postage, to accompany many of the map sheets. Agricultural Land Classification Maps are obtainable from HMSO and you can obtain a complete list of the sheets from HMSO (ask for Sectional List 1, which is free) or from the Publications Division of the Ministry of Agriculture, Fisheries and Food (see p. 189 for the address). The Ministry will also supply the maps and reports direct. Alternatively, you can ask at the nearest office of the Ministry, which is listed in the telephone directory and at the post office, and there will be an official who probably can tell you the classification of any particular piece of land.

Types of farms

The farms of Britain can be divided into broad categories; and if you know the type of farm you are buying you will know quite a lot about the environmental conditions under which it operates.

There are ten main types. Hill sheep farming is practised on the rough grazing of the uplands. It is based on the hill and mountain

15

breeds of sheep (eg, Scotch Blackface, Herdwick, Derbyshire Gritstone, Cheviot, etc) which are managed extensively. Many farms have access to common grazing on the higher ground. The main products are wether sheep (ie, castrated male lambs that have been weaned but have not been shorn for the first time) sold as store lambs for fattening in more lowland areas or, if the pasture is good enough, sold as fat lambs for slaughter; cast ewes (five or six years old) that are sold for cross-breeding most commonly with a Border Leicester ram; surplus ewe lambs sold for breeding, and wool. Hill sheep farming may be combined with beef cattle based on the hardier breeds such as Galloway or Welsh Black, which may be crossed with Hereford or Shorthorn. In parts of Scotland you will still see Highland cattle, which also live on hill farms and are killed for beef. The cows are mated in midsummer, wintered indoors, and calve in the spring. The calves remain with their dams until the autumn, when they are sold for fattening in the lowlands. There may be some competition between the sheep and cattle in early spring and in autumn, but generally cattle and sheep complement one another well. Their feeding habits being different (cattle tear off clumps of long grass, while sheep nibble at short grass), the more efficient grazing can improve pastures. If you have a small hill farm, with grazing rights on common land, it is worth considering stocking with both species. Hill farming can also combine well with forestry if the farm includes tracts that cannot be farmed economically. Forestry does not have to consist of vast areas of conifer stands as it can be managed on a much smaller scale.

At a rather lower altitude and in the north where the climate is similar to that on the lower hills, cattle are raised. In much of Britain the specialised beef herd has vanished, to be replaced by dairy cattle which are crossed with beef breeds so that calves from the dairy herd can be raised for beef. However, this regime pre-supposes land suitable for dairying and on the higher ground and poorer pastures, dairying may not be practicable on any scale. You will see Aberdeen Angus, Beef Shorthorn, Welsh Black, Galloway or, on the better land, Hereford beef animals. These may be pure bred or crossed—you will see increasing evidence of Charolais

16

blood and now and then pure-bred Charolais animals. On the better land some dairying is possible, based usually on Ayrshire cattle and sometimes British Friesians. Land that can support cattle can usually be persuaded to support a couple of house cows, of course. This kind of cattle farming may finish animals for beef or produce calves for fattening in the lowlands. Sheep are also important on such farms, but conditions being more favourable than in the highlands, lambs can be fattened ready for slaughter. The sheep income is derived from the sale of fat wether lambs, ewe lambs for breeding, cast ewes for crossing, or draft (ie, cull) ewes that will be killed for mutton. Typically, the hill sheep breeds are sold for crossing with longwool breeds such as Border Leicester that are kept on the lower farms. Animals sold off these lower farms are commonly crossed with a true lowland breed.

At a lower altitude still are the farms where cattle and sheep are fattened for meat. Fodder crops can be grown, so that in terms of land classification, the land is entering Grade 3, and dairying may be practicable on the better land.

Lowland farms that are limited climatically in respect of the crops they will grow, but that produce good grass, are most commonly used for dairying, perhaps combined with a little beef fattening. Apart from the milk itself, calves are the most important product of dairy farms.

On good Grade 3 land you may still find, and can still practise, mixed farming. At one time this was believed to be the most advanced kind of farming and the great improvements in arable cropping and livestock husbandry that began in the eighteenth century were based on mixed farms. A mixed farm carries cattle, often lowland breeds of sheep, grows forage and root crops, and grows cereals, some of which are sold for human consumption. The precise balance of enterprises depends on local circumstances, but it will fall under one of four headings: mixed dairying and beef with hill sheep; mixed dairying and arable farming; mixed dairying, beef and sheep fattening and arable farming; or mixed beef and sheep fattening with arable farming.

The last two types of farm are the mainly arable farm which these days may include no livestock at all; and horticultural farms, with or without a few animals, that includes market gardening and fruit growing.

How good is the land?

While farms fall into broad types which are distributed according to a clear geographical pattern, it is often possible to extend the range of enterprises which land will sustain. This is especially true of small areas, where investment and management are concentrated. Where the dominant farming pattern is typical of the hills, for example, you will often find that a vegetable garden flourishes beside the farmhouse. It flourishes because a great deal of work was expended in preparing and developing a fertile soil and, probably, a sheltered situation. It does mean, though, that vegetables could be grown on a larger scale if the ground could be prepared.

There is no difficulty in recognising a prosperous, well-managed farm; but it requires more imagination to see the potential in land that is run down, infested with weeds, or badly drained. Unless you have considerable farming experience, it is a good idea to visit such farms in the company of someone whose judgement you respect and whose professional knowledge will help you to assess them.

Beware of the north-facing side of steep-sided east-west valleys. It is possible that they will never experience direct sunlight, and as a result, they will be colder than they should be for their latitude and altitude.

Beware of frost hollows in valley bottoms, where horticulture may not be possible if there is competition from frost-free holdings nearby.

Beware of low-lying land close to a river. If it is obviously wet, with water lying on the surface, or reed or sedges typical of a wet habitat, it may not be possible to drain. It could be lying so close to the water table that it floods regularly, and there may be no lower level to which the surplus water can be carried. Even when it is dry enough to bear the weight of livestock, the grazing will be poor and possibly infested with liver fluke, so that stock will not thrive on it.

Land that is wet but above river level can be drained, but the need for drainage may not be apparent, especially if you see the land in summer after a spell of dry weather. On pasture land, look for a thin cover of grass with patches of bare ground, and watch for shallow-rooting, creeping types of grass. If you can pull up a handful of grass and see that its roots penetrate only an inch or two, this can indicate poor drainage. The land may look very dry as though affected by drought. This, too, is a sign of poor drainage. If the water table approaches very close to the surface at some times of the year, crops will form shallow roots to reach the water. When the water table falls, the root system will prove insufficient, and crops will be retarded or even die. You will be able to judge the situation better if you can see a soil profile. For this a hole about three feet deep will need to be dug in order to expose a vertical face. If the soil is well drained, it should be coloured evenly in various shades of browns. If it is black, dark grey, or blue at any level, then it may be waterlogged more or less permanently. If it is mottled, with rust-coloured patches, then it may be waterlogged at some times of the year. If the profile reveals a compacted, or structureless layer, which may be rust-coloured, this is a 'pan' and it will cause drainage problems and shallow rooting, though it may be possible to break it by nothing more complicated than deep ploughing.

The Ministry of Agriculture, Fisheries and Food publishes a series of excellent leaflets on land drainage. There are 18 leaflets in all, obtainable free from the Ministry (see p. 189 for the address). When examining a farm for the first time it might be a good idea to take with you leaflet One: *Does Your Land Need Drainage?*

If the land does require draining and it can be done, this may prove expensive. It may be that no more is needed than the clearing out of old ditches or the digging of new ones; but if more expensive treatment is required, the making of mole drains or the laying of tile drains should be undertaken by a contractor who will have the powerful equipment that is required. On farms that qualify for official support, a grant is payable for the capital cost of installing drainage equal to half the actual cost, and in the case of hill farms equal to 60 per cent of the actual cost.

If the land is well drained and the soil structure good, problems of poor fertility are not serious, although they can be expensive to remedy. Fields that are badly infested with weeds may be deficient in plant nutrients, allowing the more opportunist, less demanding, plant species to flourish at the expense of the 'hungrier' crops. Some weeds indicate fertility, however. Good, large thistles are a healthy sign, as are stinging nettles. Probably the most common fault on British farmland is excess acidity. Because they are inherently acid, or because many years of cropping have removed the calcium that once neutralised the soil acids, the pH of soils falls, and one by one crops fail and weeds invade. This problem is remedied quickly and simply by the application of agricultural lime. Shortages of particular plant nutrients are remedied by applying the appropriate fertiliser. The pH and nutrient status of a soil are determined by tests. The pH test is rough and ready, but simple and quick. Fuller analyses are rather more complex. Advice on soil fertility and, where necessary, soil tests, can be obtained from ADAS (the Agricultural Development and Advisory Service) whose address is to be found in the telephone directory and at post offices.

Fertiliser manufacturers also provide advice on soils and will perform tests. But although these companies should be impartial, they do have an interest in selling fertilisers; and it is at least possible that they may exaggerate problems or propose remedies that are more expensive than is strictly necessary.

What is good soil?

The short answer is that there is no such thing. Provided the land has soil and is not composed of outcropping rock, and provided it is not waterlogged, most soils can be used, and for some crops the very rich, fertile soils are actually harmful.

Pedology, the science of soils, is a branch of the earth sciences that classifies soils into many types. If you were considering the purchase of land for farming in another part of the world under quite different climatic conditions from those of Britain, then a knowledge of the name of the soil type in that area would be useful, as a general guide to its composition and history. In any case, the subject is interesting and it can do no harm to acquire some familiarity with the geology of soils if you plan to spend the rest of your life earning your living from them. There are several good introductory textbooks. One of the best, especially for use in Britain, is *Soil Geography* by James G. Cruikshank, published by David & Charles.

You will have to reckon with a tongue-twisting terminology, complicated by the fact that for many years Russian scientists dominated the discipline and, naturally, used Russian words as the roots from which soil types were named. More recently their work has been superceded by American scientists who have devised a new system of classification, and a new set of names that do not coincide with the old names but sometimes overlap them. Most of the modern books on pedology are American.

For practical purposes in Britain, the principles are not very difficult. More than 90 per cent of most soils consists of mineral particles formed from weathered rock, and it is the size of these particles that gives the soil its particular characteristics. The largest particles are called 'sand'. A sandy soil is light but may be rather structureless because the particles are, by and large, too big to adhere to one another so that the whole mass tends to settle in an homogenous way. Sandy soils drain well, which is both an advantage and a disadvantage. They are not prone to waterlogging and they dry out well early in the year, so that early cultivation is not delayed. In dry weather, however, they do not retain moisture well and fertiliser applied when the soil is dry may be leached out (ie, washed away) rapidly if the dry spell is followed by heavy rain. Because they are light and dry, sandy soils warm quickly in the spring, which helps the early germination of seed. This is a most important advantage in horticulture, where market prices are much higher for produce that arrives before the main glut. If you have a chance to buy a holding with sandy soil on a south or south–west facing slope, then horticulture may be the most profitable enterprise for you.

At the other extreme, the smallest soil particles are called 'clay'. They stick to one another to give a heavy soil that is difficult to work. A clay soil holds moisture and may require draining to remove the surplus, but it is less likely to be affected by drought. Because it is wet it warms slowly in spring and cools slowly in autumn, so that it produces late crops.

Most soils are neither pure sand nor pure clay, but are composed of a mixture of the two, together with greater or lesser amounts of silt, chalk derived from underlying rock, and humus which is the end product of the decomposition of organic residues. These organic materials began as animal manures and as the remains of plants and animals that had died. Soil that is neither very heavy nor very light is called 'loam'.

The amount of chalk, or lime, in a soil is important. The sandier a soil, the fewer the plant nutrients it is likely to contain. Conversely, a heavy clay soil may be very rich in nutrients, provided these can be made available to plants. In moderate amounts, both soils will compensate for calcium removed by cropping so that the farmed land tends to maintain a pH of around 7.0 (neutrality), which favours a large range of crops. If the soil is deficient in chalk, then regular liming may be necessary to prevent the pH from falling too far. If the land contains too much chalk, however, it may be inherently alkaline, and this is more difficult to remedy. In practice, the farming has to be tailored to suit the soil. Very calcareous soils, such as those of the Downs, Cotswolds, Chilterns and areas in the Pennines, have to be managed with special care because they are liable to lose their structure entirely if they are worked when wet, so that on drying they set very hard.

Most peat soils are very infertile, despite the fact that they are composed almost entirely of organic matter. They are black in colour, usually waterlogged and very acid. Peat is formed by the incomplete decomposition of plant remains under the anaerobic conditions caused by water-logging. Where peat bogs are deep enough to compress the lower layers, the peat is valuable for fuel, but otherwise such areas are of no great use to the farmer though they are very valuable to the naturalist. In a few areas, however, the peat has been drained thoroughly, its acidity remedied, and cultivated to make the most fertile of all soils. These rich peat soils are found mainly in the fens of South Yorkshire, Lincolnshire, Norfolk and Cambridgeshire. They are a diminishing asset because the exposure of partly decomposed organic matter to the air permits rapid oxidation to complete the process of decomposition, so that the soils reduce in volume.

Downland soils, overlying chalk, are thin. This is an important limiting factor to the crops that can be grown on them, and the depth of a soil is as important as its mineral composition. Many crops root to a depth of several feet and they cannot be grown successfully on soil that does not provide adequate depth, regardless of the availability of nutrients and water.

Farming modifies soils greatly, so that few agricultural soils retain their original characteristics entirely. Heavy clay can be ameliorated by the addition of sand; very light sand will develop a more satisfactory structure by regular application of organic materials. Grass will produce a dense mat of root fibres that are left behind to improve the structure of the soil after the grassland has been ploughed. Deep-rooting plants will penetrate even the heaviest land and when the plants are removed parts of the roots will remain in the soil to decompose and leave channels through which water can move. In a word, there are few problems that cannot be overcome in time, provided there is some kind of soil with which to work.

How much land do you need?

There is no single, simple answer for people who wish, or need, to know the minimum area of land that will provide them with a living. The question is asked frequently by those drawn towards the self-sufficient way of life, for whom the production requirement is easier to define, but still the answer cannot be simple. People are usually told to allow a minimum of five acres—which should feed a family of four—and thereafter to allow one acre for each additional person. As a rule of thumb this may be helpful, but you must remember that five acres of mountain top in Sutherland is very different from five acres of Cambridgeshire fen. There is no answer.

For a smallholder, the solution is to turn the question around. Given a particular acreage, of a particular soil in a particular situation and locality, how can it be managed most profitably? This question can be answered, at least in general terms. It is possible to set fairly realistic minima to the size of economic enterprises and to relate this to acreages, provided we remember that there are many people who make an adequate living out of 40 acres or less and as many more who cannot make a living out of 100 acres of similar land.

Arable farms are measured in hundreds of acres and a large arable farm may extend to 1,000 acres or more. Two thousand-acre farms are not uncommon. When you consider that a milking cow costs a great deal more than a bag of seed, it seems strange that arable farming should be the branch of farming that requires the highest capital investment, yet this is a fact. It is also the least restricting branch of farming, in the sense that the arable farmer can go away on holiday and leave his crops to grow by themselves. The dairy farmer cannot leave even for a day without organising a relief to see to the milking; and although a beef or sheep farmer can go away for a day, they dare not stay away for much longer.

The arable farmer is the envy of many stock farmers. Why is his enterprise so expensive? There are two related reasons. The first is the cost of the machines without which he cannot grow arable crops economically. All farmers use tractors and ploughs and other implements for cultivation, but a combine harvester is much more expensive than any of these. A reasonable secondhand combine might cost in the region of £7,000 for a small one, £10,000 for a large one (12ft and 15ft cut respectively). A new combine will cost twice that, or more. The combine may need special attachments for handling crops other than cereals, and a baler will be needed to deal with the cereal straw. Grain must be dried after harvesting and the cheapest drying equipment, secondhand but in working order, will cost £500 or more. A grain silo, for storing grain, will cost £800 or more for a small bin (18 tonnes) and more than £1,000 for one that holds about 40 tonnes. Thus, the high degree of mechanisation requires the purely arable farmer to operate on a large scale so that his investment can be related to a high level of output and so that the machines that he must have can be used to the full. The large scale on which he must operate is the second reason for the high capital cost. Once he opts for a large acreage, the most expensive item among his operating costs is usually chemicals.

Purely arable farming is quite unsuitable for the smallholder, then. However, it is possible to practise mixed farming successfully on a small scale. Arable crops are grown only to feed the livestock and the main product is milk, meat, wool or some combination of these. Since the arable acreage is small and only part of it is growing cereals, the mixed farmer can improvise to some extent with his implements. He can buy old, secondhand equipment at bargain prices and hire a contractor to perform those field operations for which he is not equipped until he can do them himself. This requires him to be farming already, to be integrated into a farming community so that he will learn of bargains in time to take advantage of them, and to be ready to pay cash and take his bargains home at short notice. In other words, the arable enterprise is part of the livestock enterprise which provides the minimal amount of capital required for it and to which it then contributes.

It is seldom sensible to plan to produce cereals for profit on part of a stock farm. There are exceptions, of course, but on the western side of Britain, in those areas where the soils and climate are suitable for ripening grains, yields are about $1\frac{1}{2}$ tons an acre. In East Anglia, yields are 2 to 3 tons an acre. It is obvious that the farmer in the west of Britain cannot compete.

Dairy farms are smaller than arable farms. The smallest herd that will provide a livelihood for its owner usually consists of about 40 milkers. Each cow will produce one calf a year and if the herd is managed efficiently all of them will calve at the same time of year. Thus, the number of animals may double temporarily. Surplus calves will be sold as a valuable by-product and if the area of land available is very limited, the farmer may prefer to sell off all the calves and replace the older milkers by buying in new stock. On most land, a herd of 40 milkers will require 60 to 80 acres to supply all its needs.

Beef production can be justified as a specialist enterprise on more marginal lands that grow arable crops only with difficulty, so that it is barely practicable to provide the protein-enriched diet needed by the dairy cow. A fat steer will sell for about £400 and a calf to replace it is worth about £80, so that the profit margin appears reasonable, even when you consider that it takes 18 months to two years to bring a calf to its full fatstock weight. The problem arises over breeding because the number of breeding cows must be approximately the same as the number of beef animals sold each year, since a cow produces one calf every year. In fact, the number of breeding cows must be rather greater than this because the breeding herd must also produce its own replacements, and breeding is never one hundred per cent efficient. This amounts to a wasteful use of land if the cows are capable of yielding no more milk than is required by their own calves. Wherever possible the dairy and beef herds are crossed so that dairy cows produce beef calves, each cow in the suckler herd feeds two calves, and the surplus milk is sold. It is possible, and not especially difficult, to produce beef in small amounts for home consumption plus a small cash income; but the specialist beef farms are often on the large size (several hundred acres) and they are found only in poorer areas and in northern Scotland and Orkney.

You may see stocking densities for livestock quoted as so many 'animal units' per acre. The animal unit is a useful measure by means of which cattle can be compared to sheep and other stock. It is based on the mature cow, which is supposed to weigh about 1,000lb (454kg); and it is equal to one horse, one mule, five sheep, five pigs or six goats. It follows, therefore, that land that will support one cow will support five sheep. In fact, the land may support both cow and sheep since they seldom compete and can be run together to their mutual advantage.

Small-scale sheep farming is possible provided it is located in the lowlands. There the more docile breeds of animal will thrive and they will tolerate closer stocking. The hill and mountain breeds do not like to be confined. Indeed, some of them are virtually unconfinable and will jump or climb over anything. Upland sheep farming is extensive, but it might be practicable for the small farmer if the land includes grazing rights on the high pastures.

The animal unit must be used with care when estimating stocking densities for non-ruminant species as their feeding habits are quite different. Pigs and poultry (the only non-ruminants of agricultural importance) occupy very little space and in the past very small farms have generated very large incomes from intensive, indoor, pig and poultry production. The investment is high, owing to the cost of the buildings and feeding equipment. So are the operating costs, since the buildings must be ventilated, sometimes lit artificially, and feed is imported to the farm. Based on low prices for feedgrains, the large piggery, battery or broiler house made a number of fortunes, but its days may be ended. Feedgrain prices are much higher than they were and so are the energy costs that enter significantly into the budgeting of intensive animal enterprises. Meanwhile, the prices paid for pigmeat, poultrymeat and eggs have not risen in proportion. In the case of meat, this is because retail prices of meat are tied to one another, the products from the different species being largely interchangeable. If pork prices rise, people buy beef or lamb which reduces demand for, and so the price of, pork. Eggs are cheap because they are produced in great abundance and must be sold quickly, so that a rise in price that reduced demand would not benefit the producer. Pig farming is very uncertain, except as a marginal enterprise on farms engaged mainly in other forms of husbandry, and it is not advisable to invest in intensive poultry farming at present. The difficulties of the pig and poultry producers can be understood by means of the animal unit if you remember that what is being measured is not the land area occupied by each animal on the farm that produces it, but the total area required to feed it. If you import feed, in effect you are renting land, and you can have little or no control over the rent you pay, which will rise if you have to compete with more profitable uses for the land. But it is an ill wind that blows no one any good; the fluctuations that have hurt the pig farmers have benefited the sheep farmer whose beasts eat grass rather than imported grain. Sheep have become more profitable as pigs became less so.

Horticulture can be made profitable on acreages not much larger than a large garden, provided the conditions are right. Indeed, if the most modern technologies are used, such as the nutrient film technique or 'grow bags' in glasshouses, quite staggering amounts of food can be produced from an acre or two. There must be a

27

ready market, however. In most of southern England, fruit and vegetables can be conveyed to a big city market and sold economically, but there may be little future for the intensive market garden in areas that have access to no large local market and that are too remote to reach city markets without high transport costs.

Fish farming, which is now accepted by everyone as a legitimate branch of agriculture (except by local authorities who rate it as industry rather than agriculture) requires little space and it is not seriously restricted geographically although, of course, there must be an adequate supply of suitable water. To qualify as an agricultural enterprise, the farm must produce fish for human consumption. However, in some parts of the country it may be more profitable to produce fish for stocking rivers and lakes for the benefit of anglers who are willing to pay well to haul them out again!

What is a smallholding?

In the end, though, we have not answered the fundamental question: what is a smallholding?

It is evident from a brief examination of quite different kinds of farming that the terms 'small' and 'large' have little to do with physical size. A 100-acre wheat and barley farm would be very small, but a 100-acre orchard or market garden would be immense. In fact, a smallholding is defined officially in terms of the amount of labour needed to run it efficiently, according to the kind of farming practised. The concept is important, because although any agricultural holding of one acre or more (or less in Northern Ireland) may be registered as a farm, it will not qualify for capital grants unless it provides full-time employment for at least one person. Full-time employment is defined as 2,200 hours per year, or 275 'standard man days' (smd). For the purposes of agricultural statistics, holdings requiring less than 40 smd a year are not considered to be of any significance. A smallholding, then, is any agricultural enterprise that does not require the full-time labour of one person throughout the year or, to look at it another way, that does not provide sufficient income to enable one person to live without other employment or income. We must see if we cannot do better!

2 Money

Land costs money. These days it costs a great deal of money. This means that it is not possible to enter agriculture as an owner-occupier unless you have some capital, not even at the humble level of a smallholder. Not only must you buy your land but you must also buy stock, seed, fertiliser and machines and equipment.

For many people, perhaps for most people, it is the capital cost that acts as the main deterrent against embarking on a rural way of life. So before we discuss what it is actually likely to cost, it may be useful to put the high price of land into some kind of context.

Farming, including smallholding, is a business, and the land is its principal resource. Land is expensive, but so are factories, shops and offices. If you wish to start a business within an industry, then it is inevitable that you will be expected to invest your own capital. It may be that the land should not be owned privately, that the source of our food ought to be the property of all and accessible to all who wish to exploit it, but 'ought' is not 'is'! So before you display outrage at the price of land and the way it has risen in recent times, perhaps you should consider what it might cost to start any other kind of business that necessitates a little space in our crowded islands. A ten-acre farm might cost you something like £12,000, perhaps more. At this price you would obtain not only the land, with vacant possession, but also essential farm buildings and, possibly, a house. Could you buy a factory and house for that price, or even a shop? What is more, agricultural investment benefits from economies of scale. The larger the farm, the lower the price per acre, by and large. Despite the apparent high investment cost, agriculture is still a cheaper industry than most in which the new-comer may become established. More important still, perhaps, it is still open to small enterprises. There are many small family farms. How many small family car assembly plants are there?

29

This is not to say that the investment required does not present very real problems. Farming is a dynastic industry, in which holdings pass from fathers to children. For the children of farm-workers (which the United Nations would classify as 'landless labourers') and for young people wishing to become farmers, entry has become almost impossible. Demand far exceeds the capacity of the industry to absorb new owner-occupiers, and that is one reason why prices are high. We can consider later the ways in which those with no capital may overcome this apparently insuperable obstacle.

There are, or could be, many people for whom the capital cost is not a deterrent. Those who bought a house in an urban area many years ago, and who have paid off any mortgage on it, have access to a substantial capital sum. Anyone selling a (successful!) business will obtain a price that should be sufficient to buy a small farm, and possibly to equip it as well. A gratuity from the armed forces, a redundancy payment from industry or commerce, or a 'golden handshake' from whatever source, added to the value of a town house, may be enough.

If it is not enough, there are several ways in which capital sums may be borrowed. For those with still less capital there are two forms of tenancy: the conventional farm tenancy; and crofting. In addition, there are loans and grants that are available for capital improvements to farmholdings and for the purchase of stock and equipment.

How much does land cost?

The price of agricultural land remained fairly stable during the early 1970s, but it has been rising steeply since about the middle of 1977. During 1978 the rate of increase accelerated tremendously, so that by September 1978, farmland in England and Wales sold in lots of 12 acres (about 5 hectares) or more, fetched an average of £1,324 per acre (£3,272 per ha). Land in Wales is cheaper than land in England, so that this average must be below the average for English sales. You can see the extent of the change by comparing present prices with those for the six-month period ending in March 1966, when the average price of farmland in England

30

and Wales was £170 per acre (£420 per ha).

Official price recording does not include the very small acreages of less than 10 acres (4 ha) because in most cases it will be the value of the house that sets the price at sales of what may be considered as houses with very large gardens.

In England in the three months up to the end of October 1978, the average price per acre of parcels of land from 10 to 50 acres (about 4 to 19 ha) was £1,295 (£3,201 per ha) for vacant possession, including buildings. For land without buildings up to the end of June, the average price was £854 per acre (£2,110 per ha).

These averages will include marked regional variations, but the most recent full figures for regional land prices available at the time of writing were complete only to the end of March 1978; so they are useful only as a guide to the extent of regional variation. At that time the price for small areas of land with vacant possession and buildings in the Northern Region was £928 per acre (£2,293 per ha); in the Yorkshire–Lancashire Region it was £890 per acre (£2,199 per ha); in the East Midlands it was £1,151 per acre £2,844 per ha); in the West Midlands it was £1,126 per acre (£2,782 per ha); in the Eastern Region it was £949 per acre (£2,346 per ha); in the South Eastern Region it was £888 per acre (£2,194 per ha); and in the South Western Region it was £974 per acre (£2,407 per ha). This shows a price ranging from £888 per acre, improbably in the South East of England, to £1,151 per acre in the East Midlands.

How do these average prices compare to prices actually paid? Each week, *Farmers Weekly* publishes a selection of prices from farm sales during the period immediately preceding publication, and these may be taken as typical (they are included for that reason). In late August 1978, 42 acres of land in North Cornwall sold for £740 an acre but with no buildings; 120 acres in Cumbria, with a farmhouse and buildings, sold for £1,670 per acre; 140 acres, with farmhouse and buildings, in Dyfed, sold for £936 per acre; 56 acres in Lincolnshire, with no buildings, sold for £1,439 per acre; 55 acres in Northamptonshire, with buildings but no farmhouse, sold for £1,550 per acre; 68 acres in North Yorkshire sold for £1,838 per acre, with a farmhouse and buildings. Just under 30 acres in Oxfordshire, with buildings but no farmhouse, sold for £1,384 per acre. Near Newquay, in North Cornwall, a large (seven bedroom) farmhouse, outbuildings and 9½ acres of land sold for £37,000, which is about £3,890 per acre. The price per acre is clearly absurd, but it demonstrates how very small acreages are sold mainly by the value of the buildings; while with large acreages the value of the buildings is absorbed and thus the average price per acre falls.

Is there a pattern? It is difficult to detect one, but it is possible to make a few general observations. The most productive land, and therefore land in the most productive areas, is the most valuable. However, since the optimum farm size varies according to the enterprise or farm type, certain advantages to the smallholder may emerge. In the arable regions, for example, a very small acreage may be of value only to the farmer whose land it adjoins—and then only if it can be added conveniently to his present holding. Locally, it would not be regarded as a viable unit in itself, and this might reduce its price. Small acreages that are within commuting distance of large cities are likely to be expensive because they will be attractive to people with high incomes and no serious intention of entering farming for profit. Similarly, land in popular holiday areas may be expensive, although the price may fall sharply the further the land is from the coast or other attractions. In Cornwall, for example, all property is much cheaper inland than it is at the coast, which may be no more than ten miles away. For cheap land, then, you should look to the more remote, less fashionable and probably inland areas, such as the Scottish borders. Beware, though, that the low price of the land is not due to its poor quality; and remember that in terms of potential output ten acres in one area may be worth a hundred acres somewhere else.

Scottish prices are generally in line with those in England and Wales, but there are special problems involved in buying land in Scotland. Prices are rarely quoted in advertisements and under Scottish law a verbal offer can be legally binding, even though no written contract has been signed. Theoretically, a casual visitor who remarks before witnesses that 'I like this farm. I'd give you £80,000 for it,' could find himself the proud owner, and the fact that his own valuer priced the property at much less than he had offered would not help him. Much land in the Highlands is still held in large feudal estates and managed archaically, at minimal levels of productivity, but seldom—if ever—sold. The land looks empty, and is empty, but it is not at all easy to buy even a small piece of it.

Will land prices continue to rise? There has been much controversy over the purchase of land by large corporations and by organisations based in other countries. Stories of purchases of millions of acres by obscure Arabs or Dutchmen have been exaggerated greatly, but some farmland has been bought by foreign companies or individuals. This is not new (nor is it one-sided!) and whether it is significant depends on the reason for the purchase. Where the land is bought as an investment, or a hedge against inflation, it suggests that the buyer expects its price to rise. So it is not unreasonable to imagine that British land prices will rise to levels comparable to those in other EEC countries, which will mean, possibly, a further doubling of UK prices if they are to reach the highest EEC levels. Financial institutions have bought land and sometimes they have forced up prices locally, but it is very doubtful whether they have had any overall effect and far from certain that their involvement in agriculture will continue. By mid-1978 they owned something like 100,000 acres, or three per cent of all British farmland and they were said to be buying 20 to 25 per cent of all land coming on to the market. It seems, though, that the point has been reached at which they are becoming very hesitant because they do not anticipate further increases in real terms. When the value of farmland was rising faster than the general rate of inflation (ie, it was increasing in value absolutely), land was a sound investment. If this phase has passed and the rate of increase is about to slow, the investment is less attractive, and prices of £1,000 to £1,500 an acre are more dubious investment prospects. So the institutions are tending now to buy land in order to farm it, rather than simply to own it and profit from its increasing value. Most foreign buyers also plan to farm the land they buy. This may suggest that British land prices are now close to their correct level and that although they may rise somewhat, especially where the land is very productive, most future increases will be associated with the price of farm produce or, which is almost the same thing, with the general level of inflation, and that if British prices are to rise to the higher EEC levels, this will occur gradually and probably it will affect land close to the main marketing outlets much more than land in more remote areas.

Simple mortgages

There are several ways in which capital can be borrowed for investment in farming. As we saw earlier, where a very small acreage—say less than 10 acres—is sold with a house and buildings, the value of the buildings exceeds that of the land by such a wide margin as to distort the price. In effect, you are buying the buildings with the land thrown in, while with a very large acreage it is the land you are buying, with the buildings thrown in.

This means that for very small acreages an ordinary mortgage may be the most appropriate method of finance. This may be a private mortgage, arranged with a friend or relative or with some institution as a private arrangement. It may be set up through your own bank. Or it may be arranged like a house mortgage, through a building society or through a finance house specialising in agricultural mortgages. Such facilities are advertised regularly in the trade Press. There is not much that can be said about strictly private arrangements because the terms for these will be tailored to suit the particular circumstances and the personal relationship between the parties. Where money is borrowed from a bank or building society, the usual rates of interest will apply. It is unlikely that you will be able to borrow more than about half of the value of the property based, of course, on the lender's valuation which may be lower than your own and less than the price you have to pay.

Agricultural mortgages

Regardless of its acreage, if the property is capable of generating sufficient income to service a loan and to provide its owner with a reasonable living from farming, you may be eligible for an agricultural mortgage. As its name suggests, an agricultural mortgage is tailored to suit the needs of farmers and there is little doubt that for providing capital for full-time farming it has real advantages. Agricultural mortgages are issued and administered in England and Wales by the Agricultural Mortgage Corporation Ltd (AMC); and in Scotland by the Scottish Agricultural Society (see p. 189 for the addresses). Both organisations are broadly similar, but the description that follows applies specifically to the AMC.

The AMC was created by and is owned by the Bank of England and the five main clearing banks (Barclays, Lloyds, Midland, National Westminster and Williams and Glyn's) and details, application forms, and assistance in completing the necessary paperwork can be obtained from local managers of any of these banks. In Scotland you should consult the manager of a branch of one of the Scottish banks.

An agricultural mortgage can be arranged if you own the property or if you can purchase it with the help of the mortgage. The land itself provides the security for the loan and no other property can be accepted as collateral. The value of equipment and live and dead stock cannot be taken into account; and where much of the value of the property resides in the farmhouse, this cannot be taken into account either. The value of the property will be assessed by an AMC valuer, who will take account of the quality of the land, and his valuation may not be the same as the current market price, which can be affected by special local circumstances. In considering whether you will be able to repay the loan and interest, the AMC is realistic. It allows that many farmers have incomes not derived from agriculture, such as caravan and camping sites, farmhouse holidays, or tenanted accommodation, and this income is taken into account. Thus, if you were to apply to purchase a small acreage that would be farmed sensibly, the fact that you have a substantial pension, an income from dividends or rents, or that you are a film star, would be admissable as evidence of your ability to pay.

The aim of the AMC is to help farming, however, so you will have to provide convincing evidence that the land will be intelligently farmed by someone who is competent. The AMC will also need to be satisfied that once you have bought the land you will still have sufficient capital to buy the stock and equipment you will need to farm it; and, indeed, that with the aid of the mortgage you will be able to complete the purchase. A tenant farmer can obtain an agricultural mortgage if this is to be used to purchase his rented farm.

Once you have produced evidence that the land is to be farmed by someone qualified to do so, you will also need to produce some detailed information about the way you intend to farm it. If you can show past farming results that indicate that you are able to repay the loan, your chances of a successful application will be increased considerably. You will still have to complete a formidable form in which you plan your farm operations for two years ahead, listing the things you will buy during the stipulated period and the produce you will sell, all costed at current prices. Your bank manager will help you to complete this form. When you submit your application it must be accompanied by a plan of the property you wish to buy, a schedule of the Ordnance Survey field numbers and areas and, preferably, your farming accounts for the past three years.

These are the disadvantages. The advantages lie in the great flexibility the AMC offers by way of types of loan and methods of repayment. Essentially, there are two kinds of loan, short term (5 to 10 years); and long term (10 to 30 years). A loan for 10 years or less cannot amount to more than half the AMC valuation of the property. Interest is charged at a fixed rate and during the period of the loan you pay only the interest, usually in half-yearly instalments although it is possible to arrange to pay monthly. The whole of the loan capital is repayable at the end of the period. Interest rates are changed from time to time, but, currently, the fixed interest rate is about $14\frac{1}{2}$ per cent. This means that a loan of £20,000 would cost you £2,900 a year, the interest being allowable against income tax. At a standard rate of 34 per cent, this effectively reduces the interest charge to £1,914 a year.

If the loan period is 10 years or longer, interest may be charged at either a fixed rate, a variable rate, or some mixture of the two. A variable interest rate, agreed at the time the loan is made, will often be lower than a fixed rate at first, but it may rise. A fixed interest rate cannot be altered once it has been agreed, no matter what may happen. It is absolutely binding on the AMC. Long-term mortgages can be repaid in several ways. The simplest is the half-yearly repayment of interest plus an instalment of capital, like an ordinary house mortgage. The instalments of capital can be varied, however, so that instead of paying the capital in the latter part of the period, as with a house mortgage, the entire capital sum is repaid in equal instalments, the interest being charged on the balance of capital. It is also possible to take out an endowment insurance policy that will mature at the end of the loan period and that will be equal to the sum borrowed; and then you pay only the half-yearly interest plus the insurance premiums.

In all cases the interest is allowable against income tax and a proportion of the insurance premium is also allowable, so there may be cases where this is the best course for the borrower; but you would be well advised to discuss the alternatives with your accountant before making a final decision. The final method the AMC offers is to take half the sum as a straight loan, with half-yearly payments of interest only. The capital sum is repaid as a single lump at the end of the loan period, the other half being repaid by one of the other methods outlined above. Long-term loans may amount to no more than two-thirds of the AMC valuation of the property.

Like other mortgages, but unlike most other forms of loan, an agricultural mortgage cannot be called in, which means that the borrower has absolute security of tenure provided the payments are made at the correct time, the land is well managed, and the other contractual obligations are honoured. In fact, the AMC is very reluctant to terminate a mortgage and will do so only as a last resort. All of the information required of the applicant is used to assess the applicant's ability to observe his part of the bargain and so to minimise the risk of failure.

Once you have an agricultural mortgage, however, you can renegotiate the repayments, changing the method (except for short-term fixed interest loans) or reducing the repayment period. You can also increase the size of the loan in order to expand your property, provided the land itself supplies adequate security. It might do this, for example, if its value increased during the period of the loan so that the sum borrowed came to less than the half or two-thirds maximum.

An agricultural mortgage can be transferred to another person, by selling the farm, and if you should die the mortgage is transferred automatically to your descendants. A new buyer will have to satisfy the AMC with regard to farming competence, however, just like a new applicant.

Tenancies

Farm tenancies do exist; in fact, they are quite common, but they are very difficult for an outsider to obtain. Demand far exceeds the supply, so as tenancies fall vacant they usually go to the child of a farmer or farm-worker who lives locally, is well known, and has farming experience. Farmers will often give their own child a start in farming by giving him or her a tenancy at a much reduced rent. 'You take over those fields and live in the cottage, and I'll charge you £12 rent. See what you make of it.' Twelve pounds per acre per year is a rent far below the national average.

Most local authorities own farms which they let to tenants. The demand for these has also risen, and many authorities have ceased to keep a register of applicants. At one time you could apply for a tenancy, be accepted, and have your name added to a waiting list, so that in due course you would be offered a tenancy automatically. These days tenancies are usually advertised and given to the first suitable applicant.

Local authority holdings are usually small in size, between 10 and 120 acres. Buildings and fixed equipment are normally included in the rental as the property of the authority and authorities are empowered to provide loans of up to 75 per cent of the working capital required, so that the tenant must provide not less than one-quarter of his own working capital. Some local authorities have been selling off their smallholdings. The Government has no power to prevent them from doing so, but the Ministry of Agriculture, Fisheries and Food disapproves strongly. On 28 October 1977, Mr Gavin Strang, MP, Parliamentary Secretary at the Ministry, said in reply to a question on this subject from a Norfolk MP: 'In our view such disposals would damage the farming industry by reducing the opportunities for people who have suitable training and experience but insufficient capital behind them to get into farming. I would greatly deplore the sale of smallholdings land while there is a demand for such farms unless, of course, the sales were in accordance with an approved reorganisation plan.'

Such controls over the sale of smallholdings land as exist are exercised under Section 123A of the Local Government Act 1972, and the administration of county council smallholdings comes under Part III of the Agriculture Act 1970. A Food and Agriculture Working Party of the Conservation Society has studied the situation with regard to county council smallholdings and has produced a paper summarising the present position and urging councils to provide more, not fewer holdings. A copy of this paper can be obtained from the Society (see p. 187 for the address). At present there are rather less than 10,000 county council smallholdings in England and Wales amounting to about 15 per cent of all rented agricultural holdings.

The Government itself also owns some land that is let to tenants and that can be used only for horticulture, under the terms of an arrangement that began during the Depression between the wars, when smallholdings were provided to enable unemployed industrial workers to start a new life. The scheme was highly successful: many tenants used their smallholdings as a kind of apprenticeship and eventually acquired holdings of their own. The holdings were located in groups, each with its own dwelling house, and they were designed from the start to be economically viable units that would support a family. Each group of holdings was supplied with centralised accounting, marketing and advisory services, so that people could be taught horticulture from scratch and earn as they learned. Again, these tenancies are not easy to obtain but they still exist; and you can learn more from the Land Settlement Association which administers them (see p. 188 for the address).

Occasionally, you will see tenancies advertised in the Press, but you are more likely to hear of one by word of mouth. This means you will have to be living in the rural area of your choice. Some people approach the problem by finding employment on a farm and then letting it be known that they wish to rent a farm.

If you do hear of a farm to rent and wish to apply for it, you will need to convince the landlord that you know enough about farming to pay the rent regularly and at least to maintain but preferably to enhance the quality of the land. The landlord has no wish to see his property deteriorate into swamp or desert! To rent a county council holding you must produce evidence of five years' farming experience, of which three years may have been spent undergoing formal tuition full-time at a college. If you rent privately, the evidence of competence may be anything the landlord is willing to accept.

Farm rents vary from place to place and from one type of farming to another, but they are always calculated as a sum of money per acre per year. Rent controls were removed in 1975 and since then rents have risen sharply. You may hear of someone paying £10 an acre, but almost certainly this will be an old tenancy. Thus, when the tenant leaves, the rent will be increased to the new level. Rents are determined locally, by supply and demand, although it is rare for a farm to be let to the highest bidder unless the landlord is satisfied that the higest bidder is also the best farmer. On average, you may expect to pay about £30 an acre or more at mid-1978 prices.

There is very little land to be rented in Northern Ireland, where almost all farms are owner-occupied.

If you do find a farm to let, it is advisable to learn what your rights and obligations are before committing yourself. Like other tenancies, farm tenancies are subject to legal definitions of the relationship between landlord and tenant, with machinery for appeals and arbitration where disagreements cannot be settled by the parties concerned. The legislation is enshrined in the Agricultural Holdings Act 1948 as amended by the Agricultural Act 1958 and the Agriculture (Miscellaneous Provisions) Acts 1963, 1968, 1972 and 1976. The Ministry of Agriculture, Fisheries and Food publishes a booklet summarising the provisions of the 1948 and 1958 Acts, called *Agricultural Land: Rights and Obligations of Landlords and Tenants in England and Wales*, which is obtainable from HMSO. Equivalent information for Scotland is obtainable from the Department of Agriculture and Fisheries, also through HMSO.

Crofting

Crofting is an archaic system of land tenure that survived in what were, before local government re-organisation, the seven crofter counties of Scotland: Shetland, Orkney, Caithness, Sutherland, Ross, Inverness and Argyll. Today there are about 18,000 crofts and about 15,000 crofters. Most of these crofts are located in the Hebrides, although there are some on the mainland. Crofting is still common in Shetland, but in Orkney there are few crofters, at least on the mainland.

The crofting way of life is one that appeals to many young people. It seems to offer an entry into farming that does not require large amounts of capital, combined with a life in a beautiful part of the country. Indeed, it seems so attractive to so many people that there are long waiting lists for crofts, and many of those seeking them are the children of existing crofters!

There is no way you can obtain a croft without a detailed knowledge of the area in which you wish to settle. You will have to make direct contact with the estate or landlord owning the croft, or with a crofter who wishes to vacate his holding. You can do this by advertising in local papers. Once you have found your croft, your tenancy requires the approval of the Crofters Commission, which has a legal right to veto your application. They are not likely to refuse you, however, provided you can show that you intend to live on or near the croft and to farm it. They are anxious to encourage the repopulation of the crofting areas, and are generally unwilling to permit crofts to be used for holiday or second homes or for other non-agricultural, non-traditional purposes.

What is a croft? This question causes some confusion, for a croft is not like other rented farms. It may vary in size from one to one hundred acres (the average is ten acres) and the rent could be as low as £5 a year for the entire croft; but the croft comprises *only the land*. If there is a house on it, or the croft has some farm

41

buildings, you buy these separately. Traditionally, the crofter supplied his own buildings, which became part of the croft and were the property of the landlord, valued as farm improvements. Since this meant that the crofter found it difficult to offer security against which to borrow capital for farm investment, the law was changed. Today the crofter can buy, and so, technically, take out of crofting, the ground on which his buildings stand. These become ordinary buildings, valued in the normal way and, hence, his own property. So when you move into a croft you must buy the buildings from the previous tenant, handing over what is known as 'ingoing compensation'. You can obtain a loan from the Department of Agriculture and Fisheries for Scotland to cover this, provided you acquire the croft directly from the landlord and not by assignment from a departing crofter.

If you acquire a croft that has no house, you will be entitled to a grant and a loan from the Government to build one, but the repayments will usually amount to no more than the average rent for, say, a council house, and you will be responsible for maintenance.

In addition to the crofting land itself, the croft usually carries with it commoners' rights to shared grazing land or, in some Hebridean islands, to a piece of the machair—the level, sandy land behind the beach—which may be suitable for arable cultivation. The administration of the common land is controlled by a committee elected by the 'township' of crofters and the committee is responsible for such things as fence maintenance and setting dates on which stock may be moved to and from the common pastures. Several townships may also share still more common grazing land, on which each crofter has some rights. So crofting is, additionally, a communal activity.

Under certain circumstances, and with the approval of the Crofters Commission, crofting land can be sold and moved out of crofting. Where this happens the croft will be removed from the official register. It is worth studying the complex legislation covering crofting, however, because unless the croft is removed from the register its sale may lead to complications. If it were sold to a non-resident, for example, it would, technically, become vacant and the Commission could compel the former tenant to re-let it.

A croft is not and, in most cases, is not meant to be a full-time farm. In the area where crofting is practised, the main enterprises are the rearing of stock to be sold as stores for fattening in the lowlands, and the growing of winter keep. Arable farming is possible, though marginal, in the most favoured areas. The crofter must have another source of income, and financial assistance is available from the Government to establish small businesses that will augment the crofting income. For providing tourist accommodation or facilities, for example, grants or loans of up to 50 per cent, or in some cases 70 per cent, of the capital cost are obtainable from the Highlands and Islands Development Board, acting as an agent for the Scottish Tourist Board. If the crofter wishes to extend his house or build a new one to accommodate tourists, the Department of Agriculture and Fisheries for Scotland (see p. 188 for the address) will provide a grant of up to £750 to improve an old house or £3,100 to build a new one, as well as loans up to £2,200 to improve an old house or £4,200 to build a new one. These loans are repayable at a fixed interest rate of $3\frac{1}{8}$ per cent per annum. The Herring Industry Board and the White Fish Authority (see p. 188 and 189 for addresses) give loans and grants, respectively, for the purchase of new fishing boats in the 40 to 80 foot range (the figure relates to the length of the boat from stem to stern), or for smaller boats for shell-fishing or tourism (ie pleasure trips or sea angling). The grants usually are not more than 25 per cent of the cost and loans not more than 65 per cent, but experienced fishermen can sometimes obtain 90 per cent loans for the purchase of sound secondhand boats. The Herring Industry Board will also give 50 per cent or sometimes as high as 70 per cent grants and loans for such enterprises as boatyards, fish farms, or marine engineering workshops. The Highlands and Islands Development Board also provides grants and loans of 50 per cent or sometimes up to 70 per cent of the capital cost for setting up small industries, including craft industries, or for businesses that provide a necessary local service (eg, plumbing, rural transport, etc). If the crofter plans to start a manufacturing business that includes craft work, the Department of Industry can provide grants of 20 per cent for the construction or adaptation of buildings and for the purchase of plant, provided the cost of building work exceeds £1,000 and of plant £100. In addition, crofters are eligible for the full range of agricultural improvement grants, and further grants and loans can be obtained from the Highlands and Islands Development Board or from the Crofters Commission. A booklet, *Development Opportunities for Crofters*, summarising the support that is available, can be obtained, free, from either the Highlands and Islands Development Board or from the Crofters Commission (see p. 188 and 187 for the addresses) and a full list of publications on life in the Highlands and Islands can be obtained from the Highlands and Islands Development Board, price 40p plus 7p postage.

The crofter, then, is an unusual kind of farm tenant, highly protected in that provided he or she lives on or close to the croft and works it and pays the rent, eviction is impossible. Crofting tenancies can be passed down from one generation to the next. If the crofter wishes to become an owner-occupier, however, he or she may do so on payment of the equivalent of 15 years' 'fair' rent, which may be determined by the Scottish Land Court if landlord and tenant cannot agree. If the tenant sells the land to someone who is not a relative and who does not intend to farm it, the former landlord can claim further compensation. At the same time, the croft is hedged around by regulations. The crofter who buys his croft ceases to be a tenant and, legally, the croft, being untenanted, is vacant. The Crofters Commission could order that it be let, although they have never done so under such circumstances and have promised that they never will do so. In all but a few cases it is not possible to earn a reasonable living from the croft alone, although some modern intensive enterprises might break this barrier and every assistance is given to crofters who wish to start businesses.

Grants

British farming is supported by a range of statutory grants and subsidies whose broad aims are to increase the value of farmland by aiding and encouraging investment and the accumulation of capital on the land, while at the same time helping poorer farmers to increase their incomes to bring them into line with those of persons not engaged in agriculture. For many purposes, therefore, aid is given only to farms that provide full-time employment for at least one person. This policy seems harsh to smallholders and part-time farmers and it may have to be revised, as part-time farming is increasing. If it comes to occupy a significant proportion of all farmland, then it may be necessary to remove a formidable obstacle to capital investment on smallholdings. In other words, it may become impossible to attain the first objective of encouraging capital formation unless the second objective is revised to take account of non-agricultural incomes.

Several grant schemes operate at different rates for farmers in less-favoured areas, and there is some assistance that applies only to such farms. The term 'less-favoured area' is used by the EEC in the same sense as the old British classification of 'hill areas'. If your holding, or the land you plan to buy, falls into this category you should be informed when you buy it. If you are in doubt, the Divisional Office of the Ministry of Agriculture, Fisheries and Food will tell you. Broadly, a less-favoured area is located in the hills, and where the land is suitable for raising livestock but not for fattening cattle, dairying or arable cultivation.

Capital grants
The Farm Capital Grant Scheme was introduced in 1974 and complies with EEC directives. It provides monetary grants for certain capital improvements, such as: the erection of farm buildings and silos; the building of roads, yards, bridges and pens; the installation of a gas, water and electricity supply; facilities for field drainage, waste disposal, the clearing of old orchards; the installation of certain fixed plant such as milking equipment, grain drying equipment, plant for waste treatment, and machinery for loading and unloading silos that are not used for grain storage. The grant must be spent on fixed and permanent installations. Grants are not obtainable for egg or poultry production or, in most cases, for pig enterprises.

The expenditure must be for farming purposes. The cost must not be unreasonably high, and when the work is completed the business must be capable of yielding a certain specified minimum

45

annual income. There is a lower expenditure limit, the grant being available only as assistance towards very large items: But there is no limit to the number of items that can be added together in a single application: the thresh-hold does not have to be crossed with a single item. There is also an upper limit to the amount of grant aid that can be paid to any farm in two consecutive years, the limit being calculated as a proportion of the employment the farm provides.

The grant is paid in proportion to the actual cost of the work or on a national standard cost calculated by the Ministry, or on some mixture of both, and where the actual cost provides the basis the Ministry will examine this to make sure the cost is reasonable. If it is not, the grant will be based on the Ministry's own cost estimate.

For most work the grant amounts to 20 per cent of the expenditure, but some items qualify for higher rates, such as field drainage or building and plant associated with livestock rearing. In the less-favoured areas a higher rate is payable for such items as field drainage, land clearance, planting up shelter belts, installing a water supply, or constructing roads, bridges, sheep or cattle grids, and fences. To qualify for the higher rate, the farmer is subjected to an income test which must show that the income per worker is lower than that of workers in other industries.

It is important that the written permission of the Ministry be obtained before any work commences against which a grant application is to be made. Details of the scheme can be obtained from the Divisional Offices of the Ministry of Agriculture, Fisheries and Food.

Agricultural and Horticultural Cooperation
The Agricultural and Horticultural Cooperation Scheme, which began in 1971, provides grants for projects that encourage cooperation among producers. It can help towards the initial surveys and studies, legal and other fees, staff salaries, training and other costs incurred in setting up cooperative production or marketing schemes. In some cases it will help finance research. In the less-favoured areas it will help groups of producers with not less than three

holdings among them to buy tractors and forage machinery that will be used to make bulk feeds for livestock.

Details of agricultural and horticultural cooperation grants can be obtained from the Central Council for Agricultural and Horticultural Cooperation (see p. 187 for the address).

Farm and Horticulture Development

The Farm and Horticulture Development Scheme began in 1974 and is scheduled to end in April 1982. During this period its aim is to encourage projects that will increase the incomes of those engaged in farming, horticulture and freshwater fish farming. To qualify, applicants must be able to show that their business provides a full-time income for one person or more, but at a level below that of workers in other industries, or at a level that will fall below that of workers in other industries unless the business is developed. Then a plan is prepared, for up to six years ahead, showing how the business might be developed and incomes raised. The grant is then payable on capital items, for installing accounting systems, for livestock and machinery and, where it would help, free guarantees are given for loans obtained from banks and other institutions. Successful applicants are given priority in buying land from a person retiring from farming and claiming the Payment to Outgoers Grant: this is a lump sum or annuity that is paid to persons wishing to relinquish farm units that are uneconomic so that the land can be amalgamated into a larger holding.

Details of the scheme can be obtained from Divisional Offices of the Ministry of Agriculture, Fisheries and Food.

Capital grants for horticulture

The Horticultural Capital Grant Scheme is intended to help horticulturists to improve their land and buildings (apart from dwelling houses) so that with the improvements the business will yield a specified minimum income. To qualify, the holding must be not less than 4 acres in size; it must have been used exclusively for horticulture for not less than 24 consecutive months before the application; the capital to be invested must exceed a certain minimum; and the written approval of the Ministry must be obtained before any of the work which is the subject of the application is commenced.

Details of the scheme can be obtained from Divisional Offices of the Ministry of Agriculture, Fisheries and Food.

Special grants

Occasionally, particular grants and subsidies are given either to encourage particular types of enterprise or to compensate farmers and growers for short-term setbacks. During the summer of 1978, for example, the Ministry of Agriculture, Fisheries and Food was receiving claims for compensation relating to agricultural buildings that were damaged during the severe weather of the 1977/78 winter and that had to be repaired. Farmers were also allowed to claim compensation for livestock lost during that winter. Both these grants were being made under the Farm Capital Grants (Variation [No. 2]) Scheme 1978. It is usually possible for the Minister to find an existing scheme that can be made to cover such eventualities with a little modification.

The livestock industries have been encouraged by a calf subsidy of £8.50 for males and £6.50 for heifers, payable on live calves not less than 8 months old and suitable for growing on for beef or for breeding beef calves, and payable on dead calves slaughtered for meat. The calf subsidy is a temporary expedient to assist the beef sector. Unlike compensation for actual damage or loss sustained as a result of unusually bad weather, its renewal sometimes requires hard negotiation with other EEC members.

Allowances paid per head of cattle or sheep in less-favoured areas, on the other hand, implement an EEC directive and so are uncontroversial. Details of these and other grants and subsidies can be obtained from Divisional Offices of the Ministry of Agriculture, Fisheries and Food.

Although grants such as those outlined above form part of the overall programme for the economic support of agriculture, there are still more possibilities for special grants. The principles of the Common Agricultural Policy are explained in rather more detail in the next chapter.

How to expand

In any successful business, the time comes when the proprietor wishes, or needs, to expand. Capital grants from the Government are helpful, of course, but they are paid only on certain items of expenditure: generally, the expenditure itself has to be fairly size-able so that they favour the large-scale farmer at the expense of the smallholder, they cover only part of the cost; and they are not usually paid against purchases of more land. There are other ways to raise loans.

Bank loans

The clearing banks will lend money to farmers and growers who wish to expand. The procedure is routine and uncomplicated, and the size of the loan is usually limited to 50 per cent of the current valuation of the farm, repayable at the prevailing bank lending rate.

The method used in assessing the value of the farm is simple and so useful that many farmers take advantage of it in order to measure their performance even though they are not applying for a loan. Bank managers are always ready to help farmers to complete the assessment.

The method involves completing a questionnaire, and the form is fairly standard for all banks. It begins with a general description of the holding—area owned, area rented, annual rent, and area of land devoted to grass, fruit and arable crops. So valuable has the Milk Marketing Board been to dairy farmers that there is a space to enter the average value of the monthly milk cheque for the past year. Then there follows a more detailed list of the farm assets, in the form of livestock of each species and at different stages of growth, of vegetable produce and wool that are ready for sale, of growing crops, and of feedstuffs (hay, silage, roots, etc) in store. Each item is valued at current prices, the value of growing crops being estimated by multiplying the acreage to each crop by the average yield in the area or on that particular farm, and then by the prevailing price. The value of fertilisers in store, outstanding bills, subsidies and grants that are due to be paid, and other such items are included, together with the value—at current prices—of all vehicles, plant and machinery on the farm. The farmer's cash in hand and in the bank, and the surrender value of any life insurance policies are added, together with the value of any other property the farmer may own, and the result is a total of his assets. Against this is set all his debts on the day the assessment is made (eg, his agricultural mortgage is included as the next payment due, not as the total sum due over the *whole* loan period). When the total liabilities are deducted from the total assets, the result is a fairly accurate assessment of the value of the farm. From the bank's point of view, this figure represents the collateral against which it may lend, and in most cases banks will lend up to half the current value. Sometimes, where the bank manager knows the farmer well and trusts his judgement, the loan may be larger.

The value of the procedure to the farmer lies in the fact that by making the assessment as nearly as possible on the same day each year, when crops and livestock are at comparable stages of growth, it is possible to compare the value of the farm from one year to the next. This is as good a way as any of measuring progress, and much more reliable than simply looking at a bank statement! It can be used, too, to estimate what further investment is needed, possible or wise in the coming year.

Agricultural Mortgage Corporation

We considered earlier the mortgage facilities offered by the AMC and its Scottish equivalent, the Scottish Agricultural Society, but only in the context of buying a farm. The AMC will also advance money for capital improvements to the farm, including such items as the building or renovation of cottages and farm buildings and roads, and the installation of electricity and water supply or drainage; and it will advance money for working capital. The only security the AMC can accept, however, is the value of the land itself. This means that two conditions must be met before a loan application can succeed. The farmer and the property must be eligible for an ordinary first mortgage, meeting all the conditions laid down by the AMC. If you have an AMC mortgage already, of course, it follows that this requirement has been met. The value of the land must exceed any existing balance of a loan advanced against it, and the new loan will amount to half or two-thirds of this margin.

Insufficient collateral?

It may be that you have ambitious schemes, requiring heavy capital investment, and that the present value of your land-holding provides insufficient security to satisfy the AMC. And even when the crops, stock and machinery are included in the valuation it is still not enough to satisfy a bank. The result is that you have too little capital to be able to borrow the amount you need. This is likely to be a common problem among tenant farmers.

There are three things you may do. The first is to try to convince your bank manager that the proposed investment is sound and that it will repay itself handsomely in a reasonable time. If this fails, it may be worth considering the Farm and Horticulture Development Scheme. As was mentioned earlier, the purpose of this scheme is to increase the income from farms and horticultural units until they match those of workers in other industries. The Scheme requires the proprietor to draw up a development plan for several (up to six) years ahead, and it is meant to encourage ambitious schemes. One of the advantages it offers to successful applicants is a free, Government-backed guarantee for loans. Such a guarantee should satisfy a bank.

If your project is not eligible for assistance under this Scheme, it may still be eligible through a guarantee obtainable from the Agricultural Credit Corporation Ltd. This service is designed to assist farmers and growers who wish to develop their businesses but who lack the collateral required by most financial institutions. Details of the credit facilities offered by the Agricultural Credit Corporation can be obtained from your bank, or from the Corporation itself (see p. 187 for the address).

Who is doing the farming?

Where businesses work in a capital-intensive industry, there is always a danger of the small-scale enterprise becoming over-

51

capitalised, so that quite small cash flow problems mean debts cannot be serviced. All too often this leads to collapse. Agriculture is not the only victim: small printers are also at risk; and builders are, perhaps, the most vulnerable of all. Your accountant and bank manager should help to keep your borrowing within reasonable limits, but the fact that many enterprises fail suggests that not all accountants and bank managers are giving good advice and that no adviser is omniscient. No one can predict the prolonged drought that will occur two years from now (I made that up!) or the war that will cause oil prices to treble in a week. Ambition must be tempered with great caution, and if farmers are considered the most conservative of all individuals, adopting new ideas with great reluctance, we should remember that for a greater part of the last 150 years farming has been in almost perpetual depression and many farmers have been made bankrupt. Caution of this order is the product of generations of hard experience.

There is another, more subtle danger. If you borrow money, the lender will need to know that the loan is secured, and that you can repay. The need for you to prove your ability to repay may compel you to adopt farming practices you would prefer to avoid, and that in the long term may constitute bad farming. As modern agriculture has become more capital-intensive, one of the most common complaints of farmers is that they are being told how to farm by their bank managers. Of course, they are not told, literally, to do this or that, but the accusation is based on more than a grain of truth. In order to meet their commitments, farmers have had to maximise their profits by any means available to them. They have been squeezed hard. If you have scruples about high levels of intensification, based on the heavy use of chemicals and the raising of livestock indoors, then you should be wary of borrowing too heavily. Organic farming, for example, is much easier for those who own their land outright, have few long-term debts, and who do not have to calculate their profits to the last penny. They can afford to be more relaxed and who knows but that their farming may not be the better for it?

3 The Government

There is nothing new in the principle of Government support for agriculture. Over the years the support policies have adapted to new circumstances and so have evolved. Since Britain entered the European Economic Community its support policies have had to be revised and restructured to bring them into line with the Common Agricultural Policy (CAP) devised by the original six EEC member nations.

The actual conflict between Britain's traditional support policies and those of the CAP is more apparent than real, despite all the fuss that has been made about it. But the change has required us to admit that our own economic philosophy has altered. We have also had to accept that the world of the immediate post-war period no longer exists.

Until the latter part of the eighteenth-century, Britain, like most countries, was self-sufficient in agricultural products. With the change from a diet based on wholemeal bread to one based on bread baked from 80 and then 70 per cent flour, wheat consumption effectively increased, the bran and later the wheatgerm being used to feed livestock (these days they are sold back to us as health foods). We began to import wheat in small quantities, but only in years when home production failed to meet demand. To protect British farmers the notorious Corn Laws were passed. These were meant to support cereal prices, preventing imports from competing with home produce and permitting exports when prices fell below a certain thresh-hold. The Corn Laws were repealed in 1846, after the Irish famine, as a result of pressure from reformers who sought to provide cheap food for the poor, who were suffering great hardship brought about mainly by the inflation after the Napoleonic War, the French Revolution, and the measures that were taken to prevent revolution from spreading to Britain.

The repeal of the Corn Laws had little immediate effect, but as the great cereal-growing regions of North America were opened up, and then as refrigerated ships began to bring cheap meat from Australasia to Britain, it became apparent that farmers at home had no effective economic protection. Their produce had to sell in a market flooded with cheap imported food. From the 1880s agriculture in Britain went into decline and it became deeply and chronically depressed. There was some recovery during the First World War, when the German Navy harrassed merchant shipping and reduced the volume of imports; but after the war the depression re-established itself.

The argument behind the policy held that Britain was primarily an industrial nation, that to keep its manufactures cheap, industrial wages had to be kept low, and that to keep wages low the necessities of life had to be cheap. Food had to be bought wherever it was cheapest. Farmers were not especially important. Politically, power had passed to the industrialists who regarded landowners as reactionary and grasping. Thus, in an economy that was industrialising, the primary producer was held to contribute much less than the processor of primary produce. This was the 'cheap food policy' and it was based firmly and logically on the prevailing belief in liberal trade.

During the 1920s and 1930s steps were taken to begin the revival of British agriculture, which had reached a very sorry state. You could buy good land in East Anglia for £9 an acre and still the land would not sell. Farms were abandoned and derelict, the land infested with weeds. At the beginning of the Second World War, Britain was heavily dependent on cheap imported food, and mass starvation seemed very close. It was then that the first determined steps were taken to increase farm output. After the war, these policies were continued, enshrined in the Agriculture Acts of 1947, 1951, 1956, 1957, 1958, 1966, 1967 and 1969, and other supporting legislation.

The purpose of these Acts of Parliament was, first, to give the farmer confidence. He was guaranteed a minimum price for much of his produce. Marketing arrangements, some of which began before the war, were continued and strengthened to make it easier for him to dispose of his produce. In some cases this manipulation of the market was accompanied by more direct controls of production, especially in the case of milk and potatoes, to prevent glutting. Then the cost of modern farming was reduced by a system of subsidies on the use of certain materials, most notably fertilisers and lime. Finally, direct encouragement was given in the form of a range of improvement grants, to increase the rate of investment in agriculture. There were a few years when farmers were 'feather-bedded', when the results of these policies in terms of increased output exceeded expectations so that the deficiency payments made to bring market prices up to the guaranteed minima became excessive and some farmers became rich. After that short period, farmers were squeezed economically, so that each year they had to produce a little more if they were to earn the same income. They became heavily capitalised, heavily mechanised, highly specialised, and thoroughly modern. British farmers still consider themselves to be the most 'efficient' in the world, whatever that means. Before we disappear into clouds of euphoria, however, it is worth remembering that all the increases in farm output since the war are measured against the productivity of a very depressed industry. Today a wheat yield of two tons an acre is good in most areas and some farmers can produce three. The national average is rather less than two tons per acre, though. Writing in the 1820s, William Cobbett mentions wheat yields of close to two tons an acre. He considered these to be very good indeed, they were achieved only on the best land and certainly they were much higher than the average, but clearly they show that such yields were possible before the introduction of modern chemicals or machines.

While Britain pursued its liberal policy and left its farmers unprotected, most European countries were more overtly protectionist. As we have seen, a completely open market proved unsustainable for Britain, which responded by trying to make its own farmers more highly competitive against imports. It was a brave, and fairly successful attempt to achieve the benefits of protection without incurring the most obvious cost—inefficient use of resources, low productivity and high costs. In Europe, however, protectionism gave way to a policy of, in theory, free trade among the EEC

55

partners and strong protection against competition from 'third countries' outside. Despite the fears, protectionism had not led to gross inefficiency; but in countries with a strong tradition of peasant farming, problems had emerged. In France, most typically, agricultural production costs are much lower than those in Britain. Yields, too, are rather lower but it is very difficult to provide very large numbers of farmers, each of whom works a very small farm, with an adequately high income. This is a problem of farm structure, and a social problem, but it does not necessarily imply inefficiency. It also does not indicate that French farmers are using the resources available to them any less efficiently than are British farmers.

What began, then, as two radically different approaches to agricultural policy have been modified and adapted until they are fairly similar, except in detail. The real difference lies in the effect on the consumer of the change from Commonwealth to Community trading partners, a change which to a large extent has been evened out by rising world food prices, so that members of the Community pay little more for their food than anyone else in the world. For reasons that are beyond the scope of this book, the days of cheap food have gone.

The CAP

The CAP (Common Agricultural Policy) is primarily a trading policy. Its aim is to establish free trade (ie, trade with no tariff or other restriction) in all major products among all members, while giving a high degree of protection against competition from non-members as a means to improve incomes of EEC farmers and farm-workers.

The protection against 'third countries' is achieved by setting tariffs on all imports to the Community area that would compete with home-grown commodities. Britain, for example, must pay into Community funds a variable import levy for all the commodities it imports from third countries to bring prices into line with those of the EEC so long as Community prices are higher than prices outside. Exports from the Community receive subsidies to compensate producers when the price they receive is lower than the Community's, and if the price they receive is higher than the Community price, the exports are taxed.

In practice, the system is far less rigid than it sounds. It does not restrict the import of commodities that cannot be produced in Europe; it gives special consideration to 'third countries' that depend on traditional trading links with member states; and it allows many Third World countries free access to its markets as a form of economic aid.

Free trade among members is achieved by the abolition of tariffs and other restrictive practices. Since the Community uses nine different currencies, problems do arise over the fluctuations in the strengths of particular currencies. Eventually, these may be resolved by means of the European Monetary System, but until then all member currencies are valued against the 'unit of account' (u.a.), which is worth about US' $1.2, and is used like a kind of quasi-currency in all Community transactions.

The green pound

When farm prices are agreed, levels for grants fixed, or any other Community pricing or valuation is conducted, the u.a. is used. Individual members then convert the u.a. amount into its value in their own currency. The value of each national currency in u.a. can be altered only by general agreement, so that a currency's u.a. value does not necessarily correspond with its value in international money markets.

Does this facilitate trade? Yes, it does. Consider what happens when the value of a currency changes. If an upward revaluation occurs, then, for that country, imports become cheaper and exports more valuable and so trading patterns may change. If the currency is devalued, the opposite effect ensues. A country with a balance of payments problem can change the value of its currency as a device to correct what it sees as an imbalance, imposing or removing what amounts to a barrier to external trade. The value of a currency in u.a. is called its 'green' value and allowing this value to change only by general agreement is a safeguard to prevent countries from solving their own problems at the expense of their partners.

57

Some years ago the real pound sterling was devalued, but this devaluation was not reflected in its u.a. value, so that the green pound was worth more than the real pound. The effect of this was different for producers and consumers inside Britain. So far as consumers were concerned, their nationally over-valued green pounds bought more than real pounds would have done. Thus imports from the Community were cheaper than they would have been otherwise. This helped to reduce the rate of inflation by damping down the rise in retail prices. Of course, the imports were paid for not in green pounds but in real pounds, so that EEC producers exporting to Britain received fewer pounds than they should have done. The difference was made good to them in the form of Monetary Compensation Amounts (MCAs) paid from Community funds. So far as producers in Britain were concerned, this amounted to the subsidising of exports that would compete with their own produce in home markets, and they held this to be unfair. What is more, all the Community moneys paid to them were calculated in green pounds, so they received fewer pounds than they would have done had they been paid in lower value real pounds. Thus, the difference between the green and real value of the pound benefited consumers but harmed producers. The green pound began a series of devaluation steps in 1978 that will bring it gradually to its real value.

During the period when Britain was adjusting its own policies and prices to those of the Community, retail prices were brought gradually to EEC levels by means of Accessionary Compensation Amounts (ACAs) that were used much like consumer subsidies paid for by the other EEC members. This prevented abrupt changes in prices. The ACAs were phased out in a series of steps and have now ended.

Prices and produce mountains

The old UK system for agricultural support was based on guaranteed prices agreed each year between the Government and the National Farmers' Union and announced in the annual price review. Levels for grants and subsidies were set at the same time. The

CAP also has an annual review, but instead of one price for each commodity, it sets three prices.

The price below which market prices are not permitted to fall is called the 'threshold' price and it is calculated by adding together the anticipated world price for that commodity and the variable import levy that would be imposed were it to be imported to the Community. When the cost of transport between the notional farmer and the notional consumer is added to the thresh-hold price, the figure that results is called the 'target' price. This is the amount the producer should receive. If prices should fall below the target price, more encouragement may be given to exporters, steps may be taken to reduce levels of production and, in various ways, methods are used to strengthen prices. Between the target and threshold prices there is the 'intervention' price. If market prices fall below this value, then Intervention Boards in each country must begin to buy in the affected commodity to remove it from the market and so strengthen prices. Prices paid by the Intervention Boards are set as a fixed percentage of the target prices and in most cases they are higher than the prices farmers actually receive because they sell to merchants rather than directly into intervention.

Not all agricultural commodities are covered by this pricing arrangement, and of those commodities that are covered not all are given equal encouragement. For some there is a single 'reference' price and for others, such as pigs, there is a 'sluice-gate' price more or less equal to a threshold price. Some commodities, such as sugar beet, can be grown only according to a system of quotas that are designed to prevent overproduction. In addition to agreeing commodity prices, the CAP annual review also sets guide prices for some commodities and fixes rates for subsidies, import levies, export restitutions and grants.

Each EEC country has an Intervention Board (see p. 188 for the addresses of the British Board) and in Britain certain other bodies are used as its agents, such as the Home-Grown Cereals Authority and the Meat and Livestock Commission.

Once produce has been taken from the market it must be disposed of either by long-term storage or by some alternative system of marketing. In the past, Britain has been permitted to sell surplus produce at a subsidised price to old people, and for use in institutional catering establishments such as schools, hospitals and prisons. Its nature has been changed so that it can find a different, but inferior market. Wine has been converted into vinegar, grains have been 'denatured' by dyeing them and used to feed livestock, and fish has been denatured and dumped at sea.

The system has its faults. There have been times, for example, when fishermen have found it more profitable to fish deliberately for sale into intervention than not to fish at all, and they can benefit twice because it is their boats that are hired by the Board to take the surplus fish out to sea for dumping. This is, or was, a rather minor loophole. The most common criticism of the system is based on the 'mountains' and 'lakes' of produce it accumulates. Probably, the size of these could be reduced, especially in the case of butter and skimmed milk; but the significance of the surpluses is greatly exaggerated and the problem of surpluses is not new. The EEC is more than 90 per cent self-sufficient in all major temperate climate foods. Because agriculture is subject to so many variable conditions —weather, the state of world markets, crop and animal diseases, and consumer preferences, to name only a few—it is inevitable that in some years there will be a small deficit and in other years a small surplus. If the EEC were to cut back production enough to remove all risk of surpluses, in most years it would have to import food possibly at prices higher than it was used to paying. In any case it would be difficult politically to reduce output from the rural areas of Europe. It is also argued that the purpose of intervention buying is to maintain high prices so that farmers live very comfortably while urban consumers pay more for their food than they should. This is a trivial argument based on the assumption that people in rural areas are not entitled to a material standard of living equal to that of people in urban areas so that their levels of income do not require protection. It is also based on a fundamental misconception about the amount paid to farmers, which is much lower than the price paid by the consumer. If the price paid to the producer can be regulated, this provides no guarantee of a similar regulation of retail prices, which include the 'downstream' costs of transport and processing. Indeed, if prices paid to producers were reduced this could lead to reduced output or, more probably, changed patterns of production as farmers sought to compensate by moving into other enterprises. If the reduced output led to shortages, prices could rise again.

The actual size of the EEC commodity surpluses sounds very large when quoted as tons or gallons of produce. When they are measured as a proportion of total output or consumption, however, they are very small.

Does the CAP work?

In practice the CAP encounters three major difficulties. The first is the lack of a common currency, or even a coherent monetary policy. This makes free trade cumbersome to achieve and leads to a distortion of markets. The second is the nationalistic fervour with which agriculture ministers enter negotiations. Each is subjected to strong lobbying pressure within his own country and the idealism that inspires the Community activities evaporates as each member engages in hours of haggling to secure local advantages regardless of the cost to what should be his partners. The third lies in the inherent impracticability of devising a single set of measures that will apply equally over a region from Sicily to the Shetlands.

For British farmers the CAP presents special problems. In the Community as a whole, the aim has to be the reduction of surpluses and the maintenance of prices in a region that is very prone to over-production and glutting. Britain, however, imports food on a large scale and would benefit from a higher level of self-sufficiency. The British Government would like to see home production increased and farmers would welcome the expansion of their industry that this implies. Yet agricultural expansion and a substantial increase in output run counter to Community objectives. This dilemma must be resolved; one way would be to set up a model of the future that included the overall expansion of European agriculture to make the EEC a major food exporter during what is likely to be a period of sustained world demand. But so far the problem is still unresolved.

The CAP and the farmer
Not all agricultural commodities are covered by the CAP. For those that are not the British Government provides its own support. Overall, support takes the form of premiums or deficiency payments, subsidies on the cost of using certain materials and, as a last resort, support buying.

Beef Premium Scheme
A target price is set for cattle which may be varied during the year. Each week, when the average market price paid for cattle is less than the target price, the farmer is paid the difference in the form of a premium, but the amount of the premium is limited, as from the autumn of 1978, to 6.20p per kg liveweight (2.81p per lb). If they prefer, farmers can sell into intervention at the intervention prices. The buying-in price varies from one grade of cattle to another and the variable premium, set each week, is paid at one level for Great Britain and at a different level for Northern Ireland. In one week in September 1978, for example, the target price for cattle was 67.10p per kg liveweight, the average market price was 68.66p per kg, and so no premium was payable. The buying-in price was 63.47p per kg.

Further information about the Beef Premium Scheme can be obtained from the Meat and Livestock Commission (see p. 189 for the address).

Cereals
Target, threshold and intervention prices for cereals are agreed annually and growers may sell into intervention if they wish. Further information can be obtained from the Intervention Board, from the Home-Grown Cereals Authority (see p. 188 for the addresses) or from Regional Offices of the Ministry of Agriculture, Fisheries and Food or the Departments of Agriculture and Fisheries for Scotland and Northern Ireland.

Hops
A grant is paid under EEC regulations for every acre growing hops, the rate of the grant varying according to the varieties grown and

from year to year. It is paid by the Intervention Board, Reading (see p. 188 for the address).

Lamb and mutton

The production of sheepmeat is not covered at present by the CAP. The British Government sets a 'standard price' for sheep and in any week during which average market prices fall below the standard price, the producers are paid a sum that brings their return up to the guaranteed level. The amount of the guarantee varies from week to week. The scheme is administered by the Meat and Livestock Commission (see p. 189 for the address).

Milk

All farmers who intend to produce milk for sale must register with the Milk Marketing Board (see p. 189 for the address), whether they sell their milk to the Board or not. The price paid to the producer is guaranteed by the Board, but only for a 'standard quantity', a lower price being paid for milk sold in excess of this amount.

Pigmeat

No target price is set for pigmeat, but there is a sluice-gate price which is the equivalent of a threshold price for imports to any EEC country, below which imported pigmeat is not permitted to fall. Pig producers are supported internally from time to time and there are refunds paid on exports to 'third countries'.

Potatoes

Any farmer wishing to plant 0.4ha (one acre) or more of potatoes, of which any are to be sold, must register with the Potato Marketing Board (see p. 189 for the address) which will inform him of the maximum area he may plant. If he exceeds this area he is fined. Britain is self-sufficient in potatoes in most years and the danger is of over-production and consequent low prices so that prices are supported by limiting output.

Poultrymeat and eggs

There are no target prices for eggs or poultrymeat and all restrictions on trade within the Community have been removed. However, there are sluice-gate prices fixed for imports from 'third countries', maintained by levies paid by importers to bring prices up to the agreed minimum. The Eggs Authority (see p. 188 for the address) promotes egg consumption and undertakes market research as well as technical research and development, all paid for partly by Government grant and partly by a levy on chicks.

Sugar beet

Sugar beet can be grown commercially in this country only by contract with the British Sugar Corporation (see p. 187 for the address). Under EEC regulations to prevent the over-production of a commodity in which the Community is self-sufficient, the amount of sugar produced is limited by quota and the price is then guaranteed.

Wool

The production of wool is not covered by the CAP. British farmers who have more than four sheep aged more than four months must register with the British Wool Marketing Board (see p. 187 for the address). The Board purchases virtually all the wool produced commercially in Britain at guaranteed prices according to grade.

Other schemes

The EEC also provides subsidies for the use of skimmed milk (liquid or dried) for feeding livestock, for the use of dried fodder, hops, herbage seed, field legumes and linseed, and it provides market support for fresh fruit and vegetables. Details of the relevant schemes can be obtained from the Intervention Board (see p. 188 for the address).

What is a farmer?

Anyone who produces any agricultural, horticultural or aquacultural commodity for sale on a regular basis is a farmer or grower. The acreage involved, or the size of the operation, is irrelevant. For statistical purposes, very small holdings are not included in censuses, but this is a matter of administrative convenience. As soon as you produce anything saleable, you are a farmer and are subject to the rules and regulations governing agriculture.

You are also entitled to some of the benefits. The prices you receive will be subject to the same guarantees, no matter what your farm size; and you will be eligible for the appropriate subsidies. The advisory services will be willing to help you. For purposes of taxation and rating you will be regarded as a farmer, so far as your income from farming is concerned, and your property will be regarded as an agricultural holding.

You will need to register, however, and the local office of the Ministry of Agriculture, Fisheries and Food or the Departments of Agriculture and Fisheries for Scotland or Northern Ireland will advise you how to do this. As a registered farmer, for example, you will be given a number that you will use on ear tags for livestock and unless animals bear your own tags you may find them very difficult to sell, since a suspicion will exist that they may have been rustled!

What is an smd?

You may not be entitled to all the grants for capital improvements. Whether you are or not depends on the kind of farm enterprise rather than on its acreage. The purpose of such grants is to increase the income of farmers and farm-workers where this is lower than comparable rates in other industries. Thus schemes can be approved only where it is evident that incomes will rise as a result, and incomes can be compared only on the basis of full-time employment. To qualify, therefore, the enterprise must provide full-time employment for at least one person.

What is full-time employment? It is calculated that if a person works for 8 hours a day, for 275 days a year—a total of 2,200 hours a year—that person is in full-time employment. To forestall the grower who tries to claim that his vegetable allotment occupies the whole of his time, there is a fixed scale whereby the number of man-hours necessary for the efficient operation of each kind of enterprise, per animal or bird or per acre of land, is used. This means that while a 10-acre holding, growing some vegetables, a little feedgrain, but mainly grass for feeding four or five cows, may benefit from many of the supports available to farmers, it will not be held to constitute a 'labour unit' and so will not be eligible for capital grants in most cases. If the same 10 acres is devoted to a more intensive regime, however, it may be eligible for the full range of grants.

4 Learning the ropes

There is an old joke about a young schoolteacher who was moved from the centre of a big city to a village school. On her first day she needed to find out how much her class of six-year-olds knew. So she put up pictures of various objects on the wall and asked the children to name them. It so happened that the first picture was of a hen. A deep silence fell over the class. The children stared and stared in what seemed to the teacher to be blank incomprehension. Frightened, she picked out one small boy: 'Robert, surely you know what this is a picture of?' Robert stood up, thought for a long time, then said, 'Well, it looks like a Rhode Island and Light Sussex cross, but there's something not quite right about the tail. Is there some Leghorn in it?'

Anyone who is reasonably intelligent and physically fit can learn to farm, to grow fruit and vegetables, or to husband fish. The skills that are required impose no great intellectual strain, but they must be learned, and the child born and brought up in a rural community has a distinct advantage. The way of life, the activities of each season, are absorbed as part of the environment. By the time the child is a teenager, it can identify breeds of cattle and probably the local breeds of sheep and poultry. It can tell a good beast from a poor one; it can recognise the crops growing in the fields; and knows the names of at least some of the weeds and wild plants. It knows what the machines and implements look like and what they are for. The newcomer from an urban environment lacks this native familiarity and so must acquire it. It is not difficult to acquire, of course, and need not take long, but it is a serious mistake to assume that academic achievements or long experience in an unrelated sphere of activity are all that is needed. Even armed with all the rural skills, failure is depressingly easy, and the town-dweller who buys land in the country and arrives hoping to farm it successfully with no training or experience stands about as much chance of survival as the person who buys any other kind of business and tries to run it with no knowledge of the trade. It is possible to be lucky, of course. God sometimes looks kindly on fools (to the great aggravation of everyone else!) but you do not need to rely entirely on luck. Not only can farming be learned; there are facilities for learning it, both formal and informal, and the advisory services that exist to help you are comprehensive and easily accessible.

Learning as you go

If your holding is sufficiently large to require one or more full-time employees, it is possible to learn from your workers. Many farmers have done this successfully, and many very experienced farmers would spend several months learning from their own workers if they had to move to a different kind of farm or a farm in an area with which they were unfamiliar. You must make your position absolutely clear at the start, of course, and you need to have some assurance that your teachers are competent. If you buy a well-run holding it is probable that the people who have worked on it will have helped to make it succeed, so you can trust their judgement. Otherwise, you will need convincing of their skill—you cannot afford to take risks. In effect, your holding will be run by a committee of all of you, with your own decision-making role emerging slowly as you gain confidence. Meanwhile, your workers will teach you the practical skills. Close contact with professional advisory services will provide the skilled outside opinion against which your own performance and methods can be measured.

Learning by working

You can learn about the land by becoming an ordinary farm-worker, provided you can find a farmer willing to accept you unskilled. You will be paid for the work you do and wage rates in agriculture are laid down by national agreement. In 1978, the minimum wage for a general farm-worker aged 20 or over was £43 for a 40-hour week (£1.08 per hour), pay for men and women being equal in all grades. Most workers did some overtime, so that the national average earnings in England and Wales were £57.69 for 44.9 hours worked, weekly.

Apprenticeships

If you are young enough, you can become a farm apprentice. Apprenticeships are arranged through the Agricultural, Horticultural and Forestry Training Board (see p. 187 for the address) under the terms of the Industrial Training Act 1964. A full apprenticeship takes three years to complete; and during that time you may specialise in whatever aspect of the work is most appealing. The practical on-farm training is augmented by classroom training at a local college and part of your third year (or in some cases first year) may be spent undergoing full-time instruction at a college. While working on the farm you will be paid the nationally agreed minimum rate (currently £43 a week, without overtime, if you are 20 years old or more) and while you are attending college you are entitled to a grant from the local education authority. The apprenticeship leads to recognised qualifications.

Full-time education

Agricultural colleges and universities offer full-time courses up to degree level. The courses that are available are listed in a booklet, *Agricultural Education*, that is published annually by the Department of Education and Science. Young people going to college straight from school are eligible for grants in the usual way, but older persons seeking training in order to acquire a new or better job may also be eligible for assistance under the Training Opportunities Scheme, which covers full-time courses. You can find out more about this scheme from a Jobcentre or any office of the Department of Employment.

Part-time education

There is a wide range of part-time and short courses in every aspect of agriculture. Normally, these are held at agricultural colleges and institutes and courses available in England and Wales are listed in the booklet *Agricultural Education*, published annually by the Department of Education and Science. Those in Scotland appear in the *Directory of Day Courses*, published annually by the Scottish Education Department. Local education authorities can supply information about evening classes or day-release courses in their areas.

Specialist courses

Courses in general farming cover all aspects of modern farming, but for some enterprises not all of this information is relevant and other, more detailed information about the enterprise itself, would be more useful. You can obtain details of such specialist courses from the Agricultural Training Board (see p. 187 for the address or from other colleges and organisations that provide agricultural and horticultural education and training, such as the National Farmers' Union, the Horticultural Trades Association, the Royal Horticultural Society, the Institute of Park and Recreation Administration, the Women's Farm and Garden Association, the National Institute of Poultry Husbandry, the National College of Agricultural Engineering, the British Poultry Federation, and the World's Poultry Science Association (see p. 187 for the addresses).

Learning from the neighbours

Farmers are nervous people and this turns all of them into spies. They watch one another constantly and critically. The first farm to begin harvesting, or ploughing, the first to try a new crop or to introduce a new breed of livestock, will be noted; and provided the implications are not too fearful, discussed. This being so, there is nothing to prevent the newcomer from behaving in the same way. By watching other farmers you can learn what is being produced and which operations are being performed when. You can learn what to do and when to do it. Someone may have to explain to you why it is done and why it is done at a particular time; but only training and practice will teach you how to do it for yourself. So the neighbours can be of some educational value, but their contribution is necessarily limited.

Farmers are as willing as any other group of people to discuss their profession, and they are neither more nor less willing to offer advice. Provided that you can meet them socially, in the pub, at the NFU or, if you are not too old, through the Young Farmers' Club, they will answer your questions. They will explain why they farm as they do and they will give you as much advice as you request—politeness may prevent them from going further!

They are by no means the only source of local information. You will need equipment and supplies of a wide range of materials. Each time you make a purchase, the individual from whom you buy will be glad to explain to you precisely what it is you need for your particular purpose, and why. Even if he works for a multi-national corporation, he is still an individual and most probably born and bred locally. He is not especially interested in selling you the most expensive item on his stock list, unless nothing else will serve your purpose. He earns wages, has to pay bills, is usually hard up, and he assumes you are in the same boat. He may give you bad advice, of course, but he will not do so intentionally. You can learn a great deal from him, provided you remember to ask. If you know just enough to be able to ask confidently for a particular item, then that is what you will be sold. You have not asked a question. We are all self-conscious and scared of our own ignorance. All of us like to appear more knowledgeable than we are, but if your livelihood depends on it you would do better to pluck up your courage and ask 'What do I need to do this job?'

There are limits to the amount you can learn in this way, however. You must remember that everyone connected with farming has a living to earn. Like anyone else, they cannot really afford to take time off to look after a novice. You must not interrupt a man while he is working—especially not in crop growing where timing can be very critical indeed. When he is not working, a man may be glad to talk 'shop', to allow you to pick his brains. On the other hand, he may feel like relaxing and forgetting all about it for a few hours.

The more serious limit, though, is a product of the natural conservatism of farmers. Provided that you propose to farm in the same way that they farm, all will be well. But if you try to innovate, either in what you do or the way you do it, the advice you receive locally can be very unreliable indeed.

ADAS

At this point you may need the help of ADAS, the Agricultural Development and Advisory Service. ADAS is part of the Ministry of Agriculture, Fisheries and Food and it operates through regional offices. You can find your nearest office listed in the telephone directory. ADAS forms a link between the Ministry and its official policy, the universities and other research institutions and their findings, and the farmer. Its staff is highly qualified academically where this is necessary, and always very experienced. ADAS advisers will talk to farmers by telephone, visit them, and help them with every aspect of their farming, from preparing a farming programme and costing it, to telling them which variety of a particular crop might be best suited to their conditions. The advice is free, although there is a charge for some services, such as laboratory analyses. ADAS is divided into five sections: the Land Service; the Land Drainage Service; the Agriculture Service; the Veterinary Service; and the Agricultural Science Service.

The Land Service is composed of surveyors, land agents, and farmers who have broad experience of buying and managing land. In fact, they act as land agents in respect of land owned by the Ministry itself. They can help you plan buildings, roads and fixed plant, and advise you about the grants for which these may be eligible and, if you are buying your holding, they will advise you about the most profitable uses to which it may be put. They can help, too, with advice about industrial derelict land that you would like to reclaim, and there may be a grant obtainable for this, too.

The Land Drainage Service will advise about the need for drainage, the type required, and the grants for which it may be eligible.

It is with the Agriculture Service, though, that most farmers have the most frequent regular contact. It is staffed by experienced farmers and growers, each of whom specialises in particular enterprises. You can obtain specialist advice about crop growing, farm management, livestock husbandry, beekeeping, horticulture, farm machines and many other aspects of modern farming. If you telephone the ADAS office with a question about ordinary, day-to-day farming matters, the chances are that it is a member of the Agriculture Service who will advise you.

If your problem concerns the health of your livestock, however, you may be passed on to the Veterinary Service. This is the part of ADAS most concerned with notifiable diseases and with the diagnosis of obscure ailments. It is more remote from the farmer than the Agriculture Service, because it does not treat sick animals. If you telephone to ask what to do about a cow that refuses to stand up, whose eyes are closed and whose breathing is difficult to detect, ADAS will tell you to contact your own veterinary surgeon. If you tell them, on the other hand, that your cows seem feverish, and have odd-looking sores on their hooves and lips, an adviser may be with you in a matter of minutes. You have described the symptoms of what could be foot-and-mouth disease!

All of the other divisions of ADAS are backed by the Agricultural Science Service. It maintains its own laboratories: the Pest Infestation Laboratory; the Plant Pathology Laboratory; and regional analytical laboratories. Its advisers are recruited from every branch of the agricultural sciences and as well as advising farmers they are responsible for such matters as environmental pollution from farms. The staff of the Agricultural Science Service will be glad to help you where their help is needed, and your problem may be referred to them from another division of ADAS. They will perform the laboratory work necessary, but in most cases they will charge you with the cost of this. You may be certain that they will not lift a test tube until you have agreed to pay; and you may be equally confident that the laboratory charge they make is as low as any comparable service you could obtain privately. They are trying to keep the cost of the service to a minimum, not to make a profit.

73

Private consultants

ADAS has existed in its present form only since 1971. Before that each of its present divisions worked independently, and the largest of them, the Agriculture Service, was called the National Agricultural Advisory Service (NAAS). All of its services, including laboratory work, were provided free and it was larger than it is today. The cost to the taxpayer was high, about £4m a year; farmers were more prosperous and more highly educated and trained than they had been when the NAAS was formed during the war; and economies were felt to be desirable. The reduction in the service left something of a vacuum, and private consultancy services moved in to fill it.

Agricultural consultants can provide expert advice on most aspects of farming. They can be critical of official policies (which ADAS employees, who are civil servants, may find it difficult to be) and so they can claim to be wholly independent of any outside influence whatever. If we can make a general analogy with taxation matters, it is the difference between accepting advice from the tax inspector and from your own accountant. The tax inspector is highly qualified and there is no possible reason for him or her to advise you in ways that would increase your tax bill. Yet most people would prefer to be advised by an outside, and independent, accountant. The comparison is crude, however, because apart from some laboratory charges no money passes directly between the farmer and the office of the adviser. If the tax inspector can earn praise because the tax accounts of the population in the area are in good order, the ADAS adviser can earn praise by having an area full of successful, profitable farms. There is a difference!

Private consultants charge for their services, and although they may not make vast profits personally, nevertheless the cost can be rather high. They are of most value to those farmers, or estates, where specialised help is needed with planning that exceeds, either in the level of expertise or in the amount of time that must be devoted to it, what ADAS is able to offer. If this is what you need—and you can pay for it—then you should contact a private consultant. If you are deeply suspicious of advice that comes from an employee of the Ministry, then again you should contact a private consultant.

You can contact consultants directly. They are listed in the Yellow Pages of the telephone directory.

Advice from industry

All the leading manufacturers and distributors of farm equipment, machines, chemicals, feedstuffs and services operate advisory services. In most cases their advice is free, and also in most cases the adviser is adequately qualified. It is a little difficult to check on this, though, unless you are prepared to ask openly, 'Where did you go to school?' (perhaps you could phrase the question more delicately). You can be certain that an ADAS adviser is qualified because if there is one thing at which the civil service is very competent it is checking the qualifications of those whom it employs. You need not ask the ADAS man. If you retain a private consultant, you can know that he is qualified, because if he were not he would not survive within a highly competitive profession. If the company for which he works has been established for more than a year or two, you can be fairly certain he knows his job, so you need not ask. But if the adviser is sent by a firm that sells equipment or materials, can you be completely confident that they have not sent you a salesman, educated by the Sales Department, on textbooks compiled from their promotional literature?

This sounds unfair and in many cases I am sure it is unfair. But the doubt exists and refuses to be ignored. I have heard stories, doubtless apocryphal, of farmers sending soil samples for analysis to the laboratories of fertiliser companies and being given results that in fact were those from another farm in their area whose soil had been analysed at some time in the past. I cannot recall hearing of an adviser from a chemical company who did not believe the farmer should use more chemicals. Manufacturers must sell their goods, and salesmen must live, too.

Rules have exceptions, however, and employees of industrial concerns are also human beings. If you know the adviser and trust him and, most important, if you know that he is competent to advise you, then his advice can be as valuable as that from anyone else.

Universities, colleges and research institutions

Agricultural research is funded partly by the Government, through the Agricultural Research Council, partly by industry, partly by universities and colleges and partly by societies, associations and other voluntary organisations. Regardless of how it is funded, however, its workers are scientists, and are as impartial as it is possible for them to be. Approach them and they will help if they can.

The help they give is likely to be limited, however, for in most cases this is not their primary task and their budgets make no allowance for time spent away from the laboratory bench or the experimental farm. The results of their research percolate down to the farmer mainly through the other advisory services. However, there are 13 Ministry-owned Experimental Husbandry Farms (EHF) and 9 Experimental Horticulture Stations (EHS) throughout Britain which have open days from time to time, and which do maintain fairly close contact with their local farming communities. Voluntary organisations usually offer advisory services and these can be of a high quality. The Glasshouse Crops Research Institute (see p. 188 for the address), for example, is a private organisation that you can join by paying a subscription, and it publishes its findings, all of which are highly relevant to the needs of glasshouse horticulturists.

Marketing boards

There are official marketing boards for a number of agricultural products and some of these offer advice to producers. The largest and most sophisticated is the Milk Marketing Board.

The MMB was established in 1933 to rescue the dairy industry at a time when it was so depressed that its survival was in serious doubt. It worked to stabilise the market and to assist the small farmer. To this day it has not abandoned the small farmer and its local managers maintain a close and sympathetic relationship with them. The Board's main, and best-known function is the buying and marketing of milk; but it is also charged with assisting farmers with their breeding and herd management policies by providing artificial insemination and milk recording services; herd health monitoring schemes and veterinary research; and advising farmers on all aspects of farm management. We will consider its artificial insemination service below. Its other advisory services operate under the Low Cost Production Service and the Consulting Officer Service. The MMB also provides valuable educational services related to the physiology of the dairy cow and it will perform such apparently mundane functions as the testing of milking machines.

The Low Cost Production Service also offers farmers advice on farm management, including the keeping of proper records and accounts. It is oriented towards more efficient business management and is operated by a staff of data collectors who visit farms regularly to obtain the agricultural and financial information they need. This information is processed at the regional head-quarters, entered on to the client's records, and used to produce an annual summary of accounts.

The Consulting Officer Service is related to the Low Cost Production Service, since business efficiency alone cannot make poor farming profitable. There are more than 60 Consulting Officers, each with his or her own clients, and they visit farms all over England and Wales. They examine farms and advise farmers on ways of improving the yield and quality of the milk they produce and the utilisation of their grassland. They are not restricted to dairying, however, and can give advice on most other aspects of farming, including business and forward planning. The system is sufficiently flexible to adapt to the particular needs of farms of different sizes and types, and to allow for the particular needs or interests of the farmer.

The MMB advisory services are not free. They are paid for by the farmers who use them. You can learn more about these services from the MMB (see p. 189 for the address).

Artificial insemination

Artificial insemination for cattle is available throughout Britain and in most areas it is possible to obtain AI for pigs. In parts of southern England the AI service is operated directly by the Ministry and the Ministry's nearest Divisional Office will tell you where to find AI facilities in your area.

The leading AI service for dairy and beef cattle is operated by the MMB and the administrative office in each area will tell farmers how to contact their nearest centre or sub-centre. Each of these has a telephone answering machine so that it can receive messages 24 hours a day. The service works on every day in the year so that a request for AI can be met very quickly.

AI service is not free, but there are reductions in the cost if several animals can be served at the same time and farmers are encouraged so to time the drying off of their cows that their herds divide into batches for calving. It is also possible to regulate the breeding cycle of cows by means of hormone treatment using a drug made by ICI whose proprietary name is Estrumate. The cost of most MMB services is deducted automatically from the monthly milk cheque.

AI is very reliable and it has been used to improve the quality of both dairy and beef herds. Each year the MMB buys about 200 young bulls which appear promising. These animals are then subjected to rigorous testing, the number and quality of their progeny being used to determine their breeding performance. In the case of the beef breeds, the bulls are also expected to grow at a satisfactory rate and to produce good-quality meat. Once they have passed their progeny and other tests, the bulls are reared by the Board and semen is taken from them and stored by being cooled in liquid nitrogen to −195°C. Each batch of semen is examined microscopically to ensure that it has a satisfactory number of sperms and strict standards of hygiene, including a period of quarantine for semen before it joins the main store, ensure that disease is not transmitted by the service.

It is possible for farmers to perform the artificial inseminations themselves and the MMB encourages this. It will train farmers and then sell them the necessary flasks, semen and equipment.

The MMB bull stud is comprised mainly of Friesian stock because this is the breed in greatest demand. In the beef-producing areas it is also possible to acquire semen from the principal beef breeds, but less popular breeds may not be available. The MMB is well aware of the genetic risks implied by the dominance of a very small number of breeds and it has given valued and active support to the Rare Breeds Survival Trust (see p. 189 for the address), the voluntary organisation that is concerned to preserve less-fashionable breeds of cattle, sheep, goats and horses.

The Government does not have any kind of monopoly of AI services and there are private organisations that offer them. AI Breeders' Services Ltd and its Scottish agent Cryoservice Ltd (see p. 187 and 189 for the addresses) offer training, semen and all the equipment needed for DIY inseminations. Semen from particular breeds may be obtained from the breed societies, and there is a society for every breed. Lists of AI services for the less usual breeds can be obtained from the Rare Breeds Survival Trust.

Organisations distributing or selling semen for AI must be licensed by the Ministry and so services advertised in the Trade Press or through breed societies are certain to be safe and reliable.

The advantage of AI to the farmer is great. It is not simply that it makes available to him genetic material from the best stock in the country. It saves him a great deal of trouble and expense, especially if his herd is small, and his land area limited. A bull or boar is an expensive animal to buy and keep and the cost cannot be justified economically except by supplying him with sufficient females to keep him working for much of the time. If you do not have your own males, the only alternative to AI is to find a farmer who has, and to use his males for breeding. This involves moving stock from one farm to another, which, at best, is tiresome and can be done only under licence from the Ministry, and at worst it is impossible. When disease is in the area, for example, stock movements may be forbidden. Nor is it cheap, for the farmer who bears the expense of maintaining the breeding male will charge for service. Nor is it any more reliable than AI unless you can be absolutely certain of your timing.

5 The principles

Farming systems vary widely and the techniques used to produce food from the land or from fresh or salt water, as well as coping with soil deficiencies and crop disease, change as a result of scientific discoveries, technological developments or, and very commonly, fashion. Yet all of them are based on certain fundamental principles. What farmers do never changes: only the ways in which they do it.

Photosynthesis

Green plants form the base of almost all food webs on this planet. In ecological terms they are 'autotrophs', the primary producers in relation to which all animals are consumers.

They occupy this unique position because of their ability to convert simple chemical compounds into the complex organic compounds that provide food for other species. Such chemical reactions require a source of energy to 'power' them, and green plants are able to use sunlight. In the presence of the green pigment chlorophyll, and using sunlight as a source of energy, water and carbon dioxide are broken into their constituent parts and reassembled to make simple sugars, resulting in the release of surplus oxygen.

The reaction proceeds in two stages. In the first, 'light' reaction, light energy is absorbed by chlorophyll and this initiates a photochemical reaction in which oxygen is released from water and ATP (adenosine triphosphate) is formed, so converting light energy into chemical energy. In the 'dark' reaction which follows, the hydrogen obtained from the water is combined with the carbon and oxygen obtained from carbon dioxide, using the energy stored in the ATP, and carbohydrates are formed. (In photosynthesising bacteria, the process is slightly different since the hydrogen is obtained from substances other than water and no oxygen is released.)

Amino acids, the basic constituents of proteins, are then formed from mineral salts obtained mainly from the soil.

Fertilisers

Green plants derive their energy from sunlight. They are composed of carbon, which they obtain from atmospheric carbon dioxide; hydrogen and oxygen, which they extract from water; and a range of other elements which they obtain from the soil. All of these elements are nutrients and in the absence of any of them plant growth will be reduced, distorted, or inhibited completely. In higher animals such maladies would be called deficiency diseases, malnutrition or starvation.

The nutrients are required in relatively large or small amounts. Those needed at rates of a few pounds to a few hundred pounds per acre are called 'macronutrients' and those needed in amounts measured in ounces per acre are called 'micronutrients'.

The macronutrients are carbon, hydrogen, oxygen, calcium, nitrogen, potassium, phosphorus, magnesium and sulphur. Carbon, hydrogen and oxygen are supplied from air and water. A shortage of carbon can limit photosynthesis, producing a condition called 'light saturation' in which plants are unable to make use of more than a certain level of light intensity. Where crops are being grown in closed conditions, such as those of a glasshouse, it is possible to raise the light thresh-hold by enriching the atmosphere with carbon dioxide, which is then being used as a fertiliser. Only small amounts of water are needed to supply hydrogen and oxygen. Most of the water needed by plants is required to transport other nutrients in solution and to give cells the mechanical rigidity they need if the plant is to maintain its proper shape. In most industrial countries, atmospheric sulphur dioxide, an industrial pollutant, supplies significant amounts of sulphur to the soil. The remaining nutrients are supplied from the soil.

All of the micronutrients are obtained from the soil. These are iron, manganese, zinc, boron, copper, molybdenum and cobalt.

Since plants are composed of these nutrients, the removal of the

81

plant from the soil removes the nutrients. In nature, the death of the plant and its subsequent decomposition by other living organisms would break down the complex organic molecules of which it is composed into the simpler salts that can be taken up by the next generation of plants, and into carbon dioxide released back into the atmosphere from which it came. Nutrients would be recycled indefinitely, losses from the system being made good by imports from outside, arriving mainly through the groundwater, and by the chemical weathering of rocks. Agriculture alters the system by removing nutrients faster than they can be replenished naturally and it is possible for soil to become exhausted.

If fertility is to be maintained, the nutrients must be returned in amounts not smaller than those that are removed. This can be done in two ways, and most farmers use both to complement one another. The nutrients can be supplied in organic or inorganic form. In their organic form, nutrients would be supplied as wastes of all kinds and as legumes grown either to be ploughed in or for cropping, because the bacteria that live in symbiotic association with the roots of legumes fix atmospheric nitrogen, a proportion of which is released for the use of other crops when the legumes are removed or killed. Green manures, which are crops grown specifically to be ploughed in, help to improve the structure of the soil, but apart from any legumes they may include they contribute no nutrients since they are composed of substances they obtained from the soil to which they are returned.

In most cases, however, this method supplies insufficient quantities of nutrients to sustain modern crop yields, since the nutrients returned to the soil represent only a fraction, and often a small fraction, of those removed. In a modern, highly urbanised society, the produce of farms is consumed in the cities and if the nutrient cycle were to be kept even approximately intact it would be necessary to return to the farmlands all the organic wastes from the cities: the kitchen waste, plate scrapings, human excrement and, logically, human corpses. This is not done, so there is an imbalance. The matter is somewhat controversial, however, and there are organic farmers who maintain that it is possible to supply all the necessary nutrients in organic form within a modern farming system. We will consider their argument in more detail in the next chapter.

The organic nutrients are augmented by inorganic fertilisers, at least on the great majority of farms. The nutrients supplied by fertilisers in the largest amounts are: nitrogen (N), phosphorus (P) and potassium (K). Calcium is supplied by agricultural lime. These four elements are the nutrients required from the soil in the largest amounts and the first three are sometimes called 'NPK'. The nitrogen is obtained from the atmosphere by an industrial process that fixes it by combination with hydrogen derived from a hydrocarbon (most commonly natural gas, though other feedstocks could be used) to make ammonia (NH_3) or an ammonium (NH_4) compound. Other nitrogen compounds can then be derived from these. Urea is an organic nitrogen compound produced industrially. Phosphorus is obtained by mining natural mineral deposits of rock phosphate which, ground, can be used as a fertiliser in its own right. It is almost insoluble in water and becomes available to plants only after it has reacted with an acid to form a soluble salt. Ground rock phosphate, then, supplies phosphorus in a form from which it is released to plants slowly, over a long period. This can be useful, and it ensures that very little is lost by being leached (removed in solution by ground water). Industrially, however, the rock phosphate is treated with acid to form 'superphosphate', and the superphosphate may be subjected to a further reaction to form 'triple superphosphate'. Each of these fertilisers contains a higher proportion of soluble salts and so they are available more immediately to the crop. Potassium ('potash') is obtained by mining and a simple process of beneficiation.

Where sulphur is required, it can be included with the nitrogen (eg as ammonium sulphate) and the other nutrients can be supplied either in amounts that are known to be required by a particular crop, or in amounts that will remedy a known soil deficiency.

Fertilisers can be bought and used 'straight', as one individual nutrient element, or 'compound', as a mixture of two or more nutrients in varying amounts tailored to particular needs. In either case the nutrients are measured traditionally as 'units' or, where metric measures are used, as a percentage. A fertiliser unit is

83

1.12lb of the nutrient element itself. The fertiliser sack will be labelled with the number of units of each of the three principal elements that it contains if it is a compound, or of the one element if it is straight. In the case of compound fertilisers all three elements are given, and always in the same order (N, P, K), a zero being used to indicate the missing element if the compound consists of only two of the three. In the case of straight fertilisers, the nutrient element is indicated, as, for example, 'N52'. The numbers on the bag represent the amount of nutrient contained in the bag. This is quite different from the amount of material contained in the bag since the element is contained as a chemical compound whose partners are nutritionally irrelevant, and that compound is mixed with an inert substance to facilitate its distribution. The unit of 1.12lb, represents one per cent of one hundredweight (112lb), so that if units are used the numbers on the label can be converted into the nutrient content in pounds by multiplying by 1.12. The size of the bag does not matter. Regardless of its size, a bag labelled 'N52' must contain 58.24lb of elemental nitrogen. If the fertiliser is measured in metric amounts, the number on the bag is the percentage, by weight, of the nutrient element. A 50kg bag is the closest metric equivalent to the old hundredweight bag, and to convert the number on its label to the amount of nutrient, you divide the number by two to obtain an answer in kilograms. Where micronutrients are included, the amounts are given as parts per million (ppm) of the macro-nutrient elements.

Older books on farming may refer to various oxides and other compounds and may measure fertilisers in terms of these compounds. This is misleading, since the nutrients are not taken up by plants in these chemical forms, and some of the traditional compounds, such as potassium oxide (K_2O) are not contained in fertilisers at all, and never have been. The terminology is now obsolete.

The type and quantity of fertiliser used depends on the requirements of the crop that is to be grown and on the type and condition of the soil.

Organic materials are sometimes called 'soil conditioners'. Where they contain only insignificant amounts of nutrients, such materials contribute to the fertility of the soil by improving its structure, and while this is of great importance, it is illegal to market them as 'fertilisers'.

As it decomposes, bulky organic matter leaves behind small channels in the soil through which water and air can move. Air is needed because many of the micro-organisms and soil animals require air for respiration. The soil population is large, very complex indeed, and performs a range of essential functions which include the decomposition of organic matter and the release of nutrients. Water is needed because it is from the aqueous soil solution that plants obtain their mineral nutrients. Channels are also needed to provide pathways through which new roots can grow. Thus organic matter, and its absence, can affect the efficiency with which nutrients, from whatever source, are used. If the soil has a good structure and drains well, water entering from above as rain or melting snow will flow downwards to the water table, from which it will be drawn upwards again by capillary attraction, bearing a load of dissolved mineral salts. If the soil is structureless, this process will occur much less efficiently. If it is compacted, water may fail to penetrate and will run off the surface or lie in pools, leading to alternate flooding and drying out. If the soil is permeable but structureless, water will drain through it to the water table, but will not be drawn up again because of a lack of the very fine channels required for capillary movement. Soluble fertilisers applied to structureless soils will fail to produce their full beneficial effect because they will fail to reach the plant root area, which itself may be seriously reduced.

Drainage

Apart from a general lack of soil structure, the problem may be one of inadequate drainage. If soil remains waterlogged for long periods, the process by which organic detritus is decomposed will change, the soil will become acid, and its ability to sustain vigorous crops will be reduced.

If the problem is caused by inadequate drainage, it can be solved in one of three ways, or by some combination of them.

Sand

Correct   Too wide

Clay

Correct   Too steep

DITCHES

Clogged ditches should be cleared and, if necessary, new ditches should be cut. Ditches are used in some areas to mark boundaries, as 'wet fences'. In most cases, though, they exist to collect water draining from above and so prevent the water from flowing into fields farther down the slope. To drain a field by means of a ditch, therefore, the ditch must be dug along the upper boundary. The depth of the ditch is determined by the depth at which the water is flowing, and this is discovered by means of test borings. The width of the ditch is determined by the volume of water it must carry. If it is too wide, the water will flow too slowly and the ditch will choke with weeds. If it is too narrow, the water may overflow. The slope of the sides is determined by the type of soil. A ditch in a clay soil can be more steep-sided than one in a sandy soil. Ditches feed into one another, leading eventually to an outfall into a river.

Where the flow is fairly small, or where the need is to capture the flow from sub-surface drains, an underground pipe may be used in place of a ditch. The pipe, usually made from polythene, is expensive to instal, but once in place it needs no maintenance and will last for a very long time. Nor is its location restricted to the boundary of a field, since it is possible to cultivate the soil above it. It can be situated anywhere, and it occupies no surface space.

If more than simple ditching is needed, the next choice may be

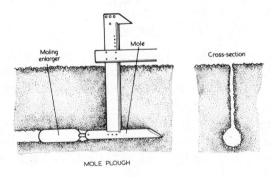

Moling enlarger   Mole   Cross-section

MOLE PLOUGH

86

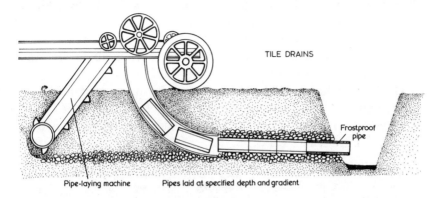

TILE DRAINS

Frostproof pipe

Pipe-laying machine   Pipes laid at specified depth and gradient

mole draining. This is the technique used where the soil has been compacted to form a hard, impermeable layer (a 'pan') a little way below the surface. Mole drains are simply tunnels 20 to 30 in beneath the surface. They are made by a mole plough, a cylindrical implement mounted at the foot of a blade that is dragged through the earth from a hole dug to the required depth. An enlarger is usually attached behind the mole to increase the diameter of the hole. The channel itself is made by the compaction of the soil around the mole and while the slit made by the blade closes as the blade passes, the mole channel remains open and a mole drain system will last from 5 to 10 years, depending on the type of soil. It drains the land to either side to an angle of 45°, so that drains spaced about 8 to 10ft apart and at a depth of 20 to 30 in, will provide good drainage.

Where the land is heavy and inherently prone to poor drainage, the solution may be to instal tile drains. These consist of short, cylindrical sections of pipe, butted together end to end in a ditch which is then filled. A tile drain should drain the land to a distance on either side equivalent to eight times its depth. A channel is cut to the required depth and the bottom made smooth, sometimes by means of a layer of gravel. The pipe sections, each about a foot long, are laid and butted together firmly. The drains are covered with straw or gravel and then with earth. If they feed into a ditch, the outfall must be not less than 6 inches above the bottom of the ditch and the final 5 feet of pipe must be quite rigid and frost-proof.

Tile drains may be laid in simple parallel lines down the field, or in a herring-bone pattern, whose side drains are of smaller diameter than the main drains into which they feed by means of ready-made junction pipes. The diameter of the main pipes is about 4in, and of the side drains about 3in.

Ditches, mole and tile drains cannot be made without using large, powerful machines that are not to be found on most farms. It is work for a contractor and it is expensive, although it may qualify for grant aid.

Fencing

Ditches can be used as 'wet fences', but it is more usual to mark field boundaries by means of fences or hedges. Hedges are visually attractive, giving to the landscape a texture that is valuable, and they are very important as areas of habitat for wildlife, often providing pathways linking larger areas of woodland or uncultivated land. To be of the greatest ecological benefit, hedges should be as tall as is convenient for maintenance (ideally, with trees planted at intervals along them) and much wider at the bottom than at the top, so they are 'A' shaped in cross section. If they are to contain livestock, hedges must be maintained by laying about once every ten years to make them dense and impenetrable, and they will need trimming much more frequently, preferably in mid- to late summer, when the breeding season for most birds has ended.

The Nature Conservancy Council (see p. 188 for the address) will advise on species to use when planting hedges, and grants are obtainable. In the less favoured areas these fall under the Farm Capital Grants Scheme and in other areas under the Farm and Horticulture Developments Scheme. The Divisional Office of the Ministry of Agriculture, Fisheries and Food will supply further details and help with grant applications.

Hedges provide ideal field boundaries in livestock enterprises; however, they are expensive, they require maintenance, and in purely arable enterprises the shelter and shade they afford may contribute to uneven crop ripening. Fencing is also costly to instal, but it requires little maintenance and lasts for a long time. It should not obtrude on the landscape visually, so that the choice of a type of fencing must be governed by considerations not necessarily connected with the cost and function. Again, grants are available in some circumstances. In September 1978, post and rail fencing cost about £1 a yard. Electric fencing makes effective stock enclosures, is quick and easy to erect, and is relatively inexpensive. Sheep and pigs can be contained by netting, costing, in September 1978, about 85p a yard.

Dry stone walling is the form of field boundary used in many parts of Britain, usually in areas where hedge plants cannot be grown. Maintenance of a good dry stone wall is minimal and not difficult, but erection is very expensive indeed. It is possible, though, that if your holding is in one of those parts of the country that abound in dry stone walls, you may be able to find someone to build one for you, or to teach you how to build one for yourself. A dry stone wall may last for centuries.

Pests

To an ecologist, there is no such thing as a 'pest'. This unremarkable fact may seem of little help to the farmer or grower faced with an infestation, but the scientific principle on which it is based should provide clues for the prevention of infestations and their treatment should they occur. By growing any crop in a dense, large stand, the farmer provides a supply of food for those species that can utilise that particular plant. The population of these species will tend to grow in proportion to the food supply; but it will be constrained by its own rate of breeding and by the fact that it, too, represents a food supply to those species that prey upon it. Therefore, the population of the predator species is likely to increase in proportion. If both populations or, more usually, both groups of populations for there may be many species involved, maintain a constant balance, there is a good chance that damage to the crop will be of little economic importance. From time to time, however, the system fails: the predators are either absent or multiply too slowly or too late, and the farmer faces a situation in which his crop could be lost.

His response will be to use an insecticide, and provided he uses the right chemical and uses it correctly, his problem should disappear. There are risks, though. Insecticides are, by definition, poisons, and some of them are poisonous to mammals. They must be handled with care and used only according to the instructions printed on the label. The application of the spray must be timed accurately and the coverage must be as complete as possible, otherwise the problem may be exacerbated. If part of the infested crop is missed, the pest may re-establish itself. If the effect on species other than the target is too great, the population of predators may be depressed, allowing the pest to multiply again, this time with reduced opposition. If the pest population is reduced, it is possible that yet another population, one previously unable to compete successfully against the pest species, will emerge as a new parasite.

Modern pest control is based more closely on ecological principles than it used to be in the 1950s and 60s, and it aims to reduce the use of insecticides. The more the farmer understands about the life cycle of the pest and the ecological situation in which infestations occur, the better his chance of controlling it. Some insects, for example, are vulnerable to chemical spraying for only a day or two, or even less, during their entire life cycle. Spray applications outside this period are wasted. In some very specialised situations, such as the interior of glasshouses from which proliferating species cannot emigrate and into which potential predators cannot enter, pesticides do not work at all well, since pests acquire an immunity to them very quickly. The solution there, at least with some pests, is to establish a pest-predator population balance at an early stage of crop growth. Work in this method of biological pest control has been taken to an advanced stage by the Glasshouse Crops Research Institute (see p. 188 for the address).

A boom sprayer can cost about £500 and because it emits a spray from nozzles above the crop it has a drenching effect, much of the liquid falling to the ground, where it can have a residual effect on ground-dwelling predator species while missing the underside of leaves, and foliage that is sheltered. There is growing interest in ultra-low-volume (ULV) sprayers which use much less of the active pesticide ingredient (one to ten per cent) and discharge it as a fine

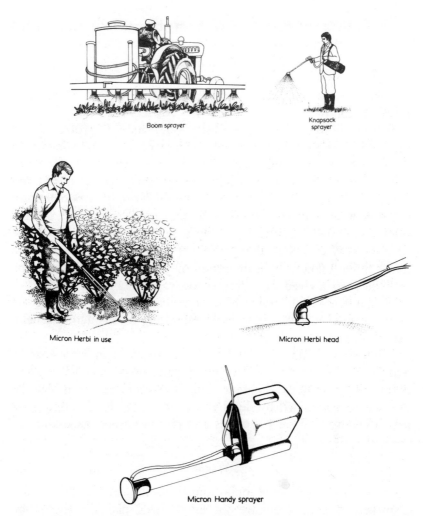

Boom sprayer

Knapsack sprayer

Micron Herbi in use

Micron Herbi head

Micron Handy sprayer

mist composed of droplets all of approximately equal size, which enter the crop horizontally, by drifting. They achieve a much more even coverage, and so more effective control for the amount of chemical used and less waste. One of the leading manufacturers of ULV sprayers in Britain is Micron Sprayers Ltd (see p. 189 for the address). It may be worthwhile to learn more about ULV techniques before committing yourself to this item of equipment, since Micron make hand-held sprayers that are ideal for use on small acreages and that are very much cheaper than conventional boom or knapsack sprayers. The Ministry does place some restrictions on the use of ULV sprayers, mainly because there is some increase in the risk to the operator who will be handling a more concentrated chemical. Details of these restrictions can be obtained from Micron or from the local ADAS adviser.

In an ideal world, of course, pests would cause no problems, and there can be no doubt that much modern prophylactic spraying is unnecessary if not actually harmful. To some extent, pest problems can be reduced by good husbandry. Hedges and other areas of semi-natural habitat are said to harbour the nuclei of pest populations, which they do, but they also harbour the nuclei of predator populations. Thus, their presence can help to maintain a healthy balance of populations so that a migration of pests into a crop is more likely to be followed by a migration of predators than it would be had the pests arrived from farther away, borne on the wind.

Shelter belts and, again, hedgerows can help by diverting air currents in such a way as to carry migrating insects across a field, rather than allowing them to settle in it.

Small crop stands are less prone to attack than large stands, and by rotating crops so that every few years each field grows plants of an entirely different type over-wintering pests can be reduced or eliminated by depriving them of the food supply they need to complete their life cycles and produce a new generation.

Weeds

Technically, 'weeds' are opportunist plants that colonise land disturbed by Man. They are not simply 'wild plants in the wrong place'. They are an inevitable by-product of farming, and it is likely that some of our crop plants began as weeds that were too troublesome to eliminate. They were cultivated and harvested instead. Rye, for example, probably began as a weed in wheat. Wild oat, as its name suggests, is the original wild ancestor of the cultivated oat; and since the earliest times oats have been regarded as a blessing because of their high nutritional value for Man and his domestic animals, and also as a curse because they were so difficult to eliminate from land that was needed for other cereals. True weeds cannot survive in an entirely natural habitat.

Left to itself, an area of land will be colonised by plant species in a succession of stages until it reaches a climax situation, a different species or group of species being dominant at each stage. In the climax state all the available space, water and nutrient is in use. There is no room for new species, there are no unused reserves of anything. The farmer clears away the natural climax vegetation and grows a very restricted number of plant species. As time goes on, the reserves of nutrient in the soil grow, since all plant species are selective in their requirements and a proportion will remain unused. This does not contradict the fact that continual cropping depletes soil fertility, since the depletion occurs selectively. Sunlight, too, is used selectively, in that crop plants of a particular species are all of about the same height. The plant breeder will seek to develop varieties in which each plant uses as much light as it can, and a dense crop stand will grow a complete leaf canopy to shade the ground. But given the existence of certain nutrients, opportunist species that can establish themselves ahead of the crop species may be able to establish their own canopy above the emergent crop and so dominate a particular area. If the nutrient status of the soil falls to below what is required by crops, so that the species grow slowly and thinly, weeds may flourish even more.

Weeds are controlled primarily by cultivation. Farmers will aim to wait to sow their seed until the annual weeds, which are the easiest to control, have germinated. At this stage a final working of the soil to provide a good seedbed will also bury the weed seedlings and so kill them. Those that emerge later are killed by hoeing. At the same time, by ensuring adequate supplies of nutrient for the

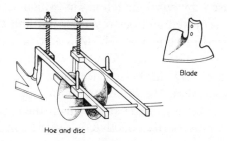

Blade

Hoe and disc

93

crop, the farmer encourages the crop species to become dominant.

The modern farmer can use herbicides to assist him. Modern herbicides are fairly selective and substances have been developed to deal with the most troublesome of weeds, such as couch grass and docks. As with insecticides, it is very important that the farmer use the right chemical in the right amount at the right time.

It has become something of an obsession to have clean fields, in which there is not a weed to be seen. Such fields look very neat and tidy, and farmers are very proud of them, but the eradication of weeds (and pests, for that matter) can be carried too far. Complete elimination of all plants except the crop species, for example, can deprive insects of any food supply apart from the crop; thus, over-zealous weed control can cause pest problems. Herbicides and, to a lesser degree, pesticides may cause physical damage to the crop plants. This may be due to the fact that a herbicide is, after all, toxic to some plants and therefore, perhaps, to some degree toxic to all plants, or it may be due to the fact that pesticides are usually distributed in an oil to ensure good dispersal. The oil may block leaf stomata, so inhibiting transpiration and causing damage.

Some herbicides are very poisonous to Man and, like insecticides, they must never be stored in unlabelled containers or within the reach of children. There have been many tragic cases of death caused by children drinking paraquat from lemonade bottles.

ULV spraying techniques can also be used with herbicides.

Crop diseases

Plant diseases are most commonly caused by a nutrient deficiency, which is remedied simply by supplying the missing nutrient; rarely are they diseased by viral infection, in which case the affected plants must be removed and destroyed by burning them; and there is also the hazard of fungal attack. Most crops are susceptible to certain microfungi and a bad infestation can cause great damage.

Fungal diseases are controlled to some extent by rotational farming, which prevents the accumulation of spores from one year to the next by removing the host on which these parasitic species depend. This is only partly effective, however, since fungal spores are carried long distances by the wind; and no matter how clean the soil, a crop in the open can never be entirely safe.

Much modern plant breeding is directed towards disease resistance and commercial seed is sold with a list of diseases to which it has resistance. The technique is fairly successful, but the breeding programme can never end because genetic resistance lasts for only as long as it takes the fungi to mutate and produce a new strain that overcomes the resistance. In practice, resistance lasts for about five or six years. As soon as a significant proportion of the annual crop is attacked a new variety must be available to take its place.

If an attack does occur, modern fungicides are very effective. Again, these are dangerous substances that must be used with care, and their use is limited. Fungal disease tends to attack mature crops which may be very difficult to reach with any kind of sprayer without causing as much damage by trampling as the disease is likely to cause. Some crops are grown from seeds that have been dressed with a fungicide to prevent fungal attack during germination and the early growth of the plant.

Eelworms

Nematodes, or 'eelworms', are very small, aquatic soil animals, the largest of which is barely visible to the naked eye. Of the 10,000 or so known species, about 2,000 inhabit fresh water, and of these about 1,000 species live in soils. They are found in the upper few inches of topsoil, most commonly in grassland, and all of them feed on living plant tissue. It is not unusual for there to be up to ten million of them beneath one square metre of surface area, and they do great damage.

Some, such as potato eelworm, are specific to particular crops, and are controlled most simply by crop rotations. Traditionally, potatoes were grown on a particular piece of ground not more than once in every four years. Today there are eelworm-resistant varieties of potato.

Where nematodes cause serious problems they can be sprayed with nematicides and it is likely that this practice will increase as only now are scientists begining to estimate the extent of the damage they cause to grassland. There may be dangers, however, in too vigorous an attack even on creatures as apparently harmful as nematodes, for although they are responsible for the loss of much potential productivity, they may also play a vital role in the ecology of soils, perhaps by providing a food supply for other species.

Cultivations

Conventional crop cultivation consists of ploughing, rolling, cultivating, harrowing and then, when the crop has emerged, weeding or hoeing.

Ploughing opens up the soil to aerate it, buries crop residues, and helps to kill weeds. Performed in the autumn, it can be assisted by winter frosts, which break up large clods of earth. The most common plough in use in the mouldboard, which may be designed to cut one, two or more furrows at a time, depending on the power available to draw it. The reversible plough enables the ploughman to work back and forth with all the furrows lying to the same side. Without a reversible plough he must work to a complicated pattern, called 'ploughing in lands'.

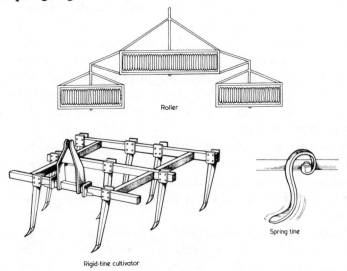

Roller

Spring tine

Rigid-tine cultivator

Tandem-disc harrow

Spring-tine harrow

Rollers, usually comprising three ribbed drums (the Cambridge roller), are used to flatten ploughed land.

Cultivators, which consist of arrays of tines that may be rigid or springy, mounted on a metal frame are dragged over the land to break the surface to a tilth. The rotary cultivator, like a garden rotavator, but larger and drawn behind and powered by a tractor, breaks up soil lumps and aerates the soil by throwing it upwards. Cultivators are also used between the rows of row crops.

Harrows work the surface to a fine tilth in preparation for sowing. There are several types of harrow. The disc harrow consists of

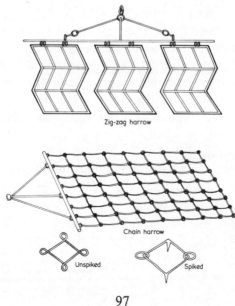

Zig-zag harrow

Chain harrow

Unspiked   Spiked

arrays of cutting discs pulled by a tractor, the discs mounted at an angle to the direction of travel. The spring-tine harrow consists of a metal frame on to which spring tines are fixed. The zig-zag harrow consists of one or more (commonly three) Z-shaped metal frames with a rigid straight or curved tine at each intersection. The chain harrow consists of chain-link matting which may or may not have spikes fixed to it, depending on the purpose for which it is used.

Weeding between rows of standing crops is performed with a cultivator, or with a horizontal hoe blade that is drawn just below the soil surface, where it cuts off weeds.

More specialised implements are available for spreading manure and fertiliser, for drilling seed, planting potatoes, and for thinning out emerging crops.

Obviously the cost of equipping a farm from scratch with all these implements, bought new, would be very high indeed. Most farmers acquire them as they can afford them, apart from the really essential items. If you have no more than an acre or two of land, it is possible (just about) to cultivate it with no more than a garden rotavator. It is easier, though, and for any larger area essential, to use a plough. If you have a plough, you will need a tractor. A second-hand three-furrow reversible plough might cost you £200 or more, although it is often possible to buy implements quite cheaply locally. New tractors are expensive and second-hand ones vary greatly in price, but you should be able to buy a small one, in good condition, for under £2,000. A harrow may be all that you need in addition and it should be possible to buy one second-hand, locally, for £250 or less. At a pinch, a harrow can be improvised from gorse bushes, weighted and dragged behind the tractor!

Minimum cultivation
There is growing interest in minimum cultivation, in which the weeds are killed with a herbicide and the seed for the new crop is sown directly, with no further soil preparation, the main advantage is speed, the farmer being able to take advantage of a brief spell of good weather to sow a crop that will emerge early. It may be, too, that over the years yields increase because of the reduced disturbance of soil populations. However, weed control can be

98

very difficult. The technique cannot be used at all unless the soil drainage is very good, and the machinery required for direct drilling is very expensive, so that small farmers have to rely on contractors, which may lose them the advantage of timeliness.

Harvesting

On a small acreage, hay can be made by hand, the old way, but it is very hard, slow work. The grass should be cut with a mower, tedded with rakes towed behind the tractor that turn and aerate the drying grass, then collected with a baler. This is the conventional way in which hay-making is mechanised. Silage is much more efficient than hay as a means of conserving the nutrients in grass, but you must have sufficient acreage to provide a full clamp or the silage will not ferment properly. The grass must be cut and

POTATO HARVESTING

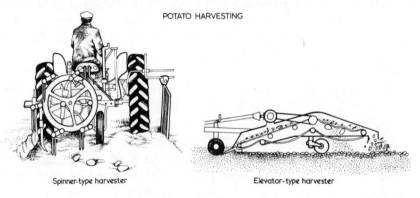

Spinner-type harvester   Elevator-type harvester

SUGAR BEET HARVESTING

chopped using a chopper that blows the chopped grass into a trailer. Silage can be made in specially designed silos, or in improvised clamps, which are concrete, wooden or other similar rigid containers into which the grass can be tipped and packed down by being run over with the tractor, or otherwise weighted.

Cereals and such field crops as beans and peas are harvested most efficiently with a combine harvester. This is an expensive item, a second-hand one costing £7,000 or more and a new one more costly still; but harvesting can be done by a contractor.

Livestock

The care of farm livestock is very largely a matter of common sense, sympathy and confidence, but there are certain principles that must be understood. In all cases the product is more stock. Pigs breed more pigs for meat, sheep breed more sheep for meat with wool as the by-product, beef cattle produce more beef cattle, poultry produce eggs which are a stage in the production of more poultry while those that are hatched produce meat, and the dairy cow must produce calves in order to lactate.

The breeding cycle is of paramount importance, therefore, and breeding females are made pregnant as soon as is biologically possible after the birth of their young. In the case of pigs, the most prolific of the domesticated mammals apart from rabbits, it is possible to obtain two litters a year with up to ten piglets in each. A cow has a gestation period exactly equal to that of a human, so that she can be made to produce one calf every ten months or so. Sheep have a breeding cycle that in most (but not all) breeds is controlled biologically by the length of the day so that they mate in autumn when the days are shortening and the lambs are born in early spring. The number of eggs laid by a hen is mainly a matter of heredity, but they, too, cease to lay when the days are shorter than a certain minimum length. This trait can be overcome by management.

Stock that is producing food at its maximum rate must be well fed, and rations are tailored to needs very closely. A dairy cow, for example, is fed a maintenance ration, which is the food she

100

requires to sustain her in normal good health, plus a production ration that is geared directly to her milk yield as so much food for each gallon of milk.

Pigs can be allowed to range free, and they enjoy it; but a heavy sow must not be allowed on wet and heavy land for fear of her becoming, quite literally, stuck in the mud. This is not simply inconvenient—it can cause serious physical injury as she struggles to free herself. It is more convenient to keep pigs in the traditional kind of sty with a small open yard in front and sleeping quarters behind. Accommodation of this kind is neither difficult nor expensive to build yourself.

Cattle will spend much of the year in the open, on grass, their diet being supplemented if necessary (it usually is) by concentrates fed while they are being milked. In winter, however, they must be brought under cover, partly for their own sake but much more for the sake of the pasture. Grass does not grow during winter, so the grazing becomes exhausted and there is nothing for the animals to eat. Thus, they derive no benefit from being in the open. Wet ground, with a poor cover of grass, can be trampled to destruction by cattle (it is called 'poaching') producing first a quagmire and then, when it dries, ground with the consistency and fertility of concrete. In-wintering accommodation can be in yards, where the animals are kept together in groups on a floor covered by straw to which more straw is added as it becomes soiled. Yards are usually covered to protect the animals from the worst of the weather. Alternatively, the animals can be penned inside a large building or, according to the modern fashion, kept in 'cow kennels', which are exactly what their name suggests.

Sheep can remain outdoors all year round, but in the harsher climates of the hills there is much to be said for in-wintering them also, in covered yards where they can be protected from the worst of the weather and fed a ration that is known to be adequate for their needs. This is especially important because during winter the ewes will be pregnant. Sheep can withstand cold, but they suffer badly from being wet as well as cold. They can survive on very poor pastures, but they cannot eat grass that is buried deep beneath snow. They are nimble on their feet in many ways, but a sheep that rolls on to its back is in serious difficulties and with some breeds it is impossible for the animal to regain its feet unaided, and it may die. Sheep occupy less yard space than cattle, obviously.

Poultry, too, require housing and they should be protected against predators, Fox, mink and, in some parts of the country, buzzards will take poultry.

The accommodation may be simple or elaborate, depending on the system of management. Free-range birds, kept in flocks of up to a few hundred, can be folded over grassland, which they will improve provided they are moved frequently. This requires no more than a mobile house and fencing. Or they can be kept in runs using similar housing and a surrounding fence or wall. Intensive battery or broiler birds, kept in flocks of ten thousand or more, require much more expensive housing, automatic feeding and cleaning systems, and artificial lighting and air conditioning.

Farmers eligible for capital grants can claim them against buildings and other fixed equipment for cattle and sheep, but not, in most cases, for pigs or poultry.

Health and hygiene

Hygiene standards for dairies are laid down by law and must be observed. They are described in the Milk and Dairies (General) Regulations 1959. Livestock being imported or exported is subject to veterinary conditions. Animals slaughtered for meat must be killed by humane methods set down in regulations.

In addition, there is a list of diseases of livestock that must be notified to the authorities. These are: African horse sickness; anthrax; cattle plague in ruminants and pigs; dourine in horses, mules and donkeys; epizootic lymphangitis in horses, mules and donkeys, equine encephalo-myelitis; equine infectious anaemia; foot-and-mouth disease; fowl pest (fowl plague or Newcastle disease); glanders and farcy in horses, mules and donkeys; parasitic mange in horses, mules and donkeys; pleuro-pneumonia in cattle; rabies, sheep pox, sheep scab, swine fever, swine vesicular disease, and Teschen disease in pigs; tuberculosis of the udder and pulmonary tuberculosis in cattle. There are also certain diseases of farmed fish that must be notified: bacterial kidney disease; columnaris; furunculosis; infectious haematopoietic necrosis; infectious pancreatic necrosis; infectious dropsy of cyprinids in any of its several forms; myxosoma cerebralis (also called whirling disease); and viral haemorrhagic septicaemia.

Some of these diseases are subject to the slaughter policy, which stipulates that any infected animal and any animal that may have been in contact with an infected animal (in practice this means all other animals of that type on the farm) must be slaughtered and the carcasses destroyed on the farm by burning and burying. Affected farms are then placed in quarantine and may not re-stock for a specified period. Farmers are paid compensation for livestock lost in this way.

The movement of all livestock is controlled and at times prohibited within certain areas to prevent the spread of infection. As the need for them arises particular prophylactic treatments, such as the dipping of sheep in an approved insecticide solution to protect against sheep scab, may be imposed by law.

In general, the prevention of illness is a matter of good feeding, cleanliness and common sense. All stock is susceptible to parasites, especially intestinal and lung worms which spend part of their life cycle in pasture. It is wise to move stock regularly so that the grass is left for long enough to reduce the parasite population. Liver fluke is a troublesome parasite of low-lying wet ground; and it spends part of its life cycle in the body of an aquatic snail. The Ministry monitors the fluke situation constantly and issues warnings to farmers when conditions favour the flukes. Farmers are then advised to move their stock to higher, drier ground. Generally, the parasites of one species do not attack other species and so different species of stock can follow one another without much fear of cross infection. Sheep are susceptible to more parasites than any other species and these are transmitted most commonly from one animal to another. An affected sheep must be kept isolated until it is free from infestation. It is said that the worst enemy of a sheep is another sheep!

ADAS advisers will help you devise management systems and treatments to minimise the risk of parasitic infestation or other disease, but if in doubt about the health of an animal or bird you should never hesitate to seek veterinary advice. It is better to be safe than sorry.

Notifiable diseases and pests of plant crops
The following pests and diseases must be notified to the authorities: Colorado beetle; wart disease of potatoes; progressive wilt disease of hops; red core disease of strawberries; and fireblight disease and sharka disease (also called plum pox) in fruit.

Wages

If you employ workers, wage rates are fixed by agreement subject to national minima agreed by the Agricultural Wages Board. The minima are renegotiated from time to time and in the latter part of 1978 the National Union of Agricultural and Allied Workers was pressing for a large increase. At that time, however, the existing minimum rates for men and women aged 20 years or older were: for ordinary general workers £43 a week; craftsmen £47.30 a week; Grade II workers £51.60 a week; Grade I workers £55.90 a week. In each case the wage relates to a 40-hour week with additional hours being paid at overtime rates, and the wage rates apply equally to men and women.

Help with conservation tasks

If there is work to be done on your holding that is of clear conservation or amenity value, work that cannot be undertaken by the existing work force, and if you cannot afford to hire extra labour, you may be able to obtain assistance. The regional Conservation Corps are groups of young people who will undertake work of this kind at a cost calculated to cover no more than their operating expenses. They will not allow themselves to be used as cheap labour, nor will they undertake work that is intended primarily to increase the profitability of the farming operation. They will clear out ponds and, sometimes, ditches, maintain hedges that are of importance to wildlife, create nature reserves, plant trees, make nature trails, and generally help with anything that increases or improves areas of natural habitat. You can contact them through the county naturalists' trusts, which are listed in the telephone directory or through their national organisation the British Trust for Conservation Volunteers (see p. 187 for the address).

6 The other point of view

It was Hegel who made much of the view that each thesis generates its own antithesis, each trend its counter-trend. Whether or not this is true in the world at large you must judge for yourself, but it is certainly true in farming and gardening. 'Modern' techniques have revolutionised the industry, but they have been accompanied by a counter-revolution. The use of large, heavy machines has been criticised severely, and the use of agricultural chemicals has been shunned by those who would produce and market 'organically grown' foods.

A few years ago it was being said that the mechanisation of food production would proceed to the stage at which any operation that could not be mechanised would not be performed at all, workers would be more or less dispensed with, and the farmer would spend his working hours sitting at a computer console pressing the buttons that relay his instructions to automated machines. Scientists were presenting papers describing such a kind of farming at important conferences. At the same time, the opposition was saying that because of their high capital and energy cost, large machines would become obsolete in the near future. They are inefficient, because the number of operations each machine can perform is very small, so that each machine must spend much of the year lying idle. Large machines are heavy and thus damage the structure of the soil in ways that may be expensive to remedy. A man sitting high off the ground on the seat of a tractor does not have that close contact with the earth and with the crop that a man has when he is on foot, so his observation is less acute. Machines make it more likely that cultivations will become generalised as the average of what is needed, so that areas requiring treatment to either side of this average will be dealt with inadequately or inappropriately.

The arguments over the use of chemicals became much more

emotional. Chemists dominated agricultural science for several years and a view of agricultural science percolated down to the popular level in the form of an extreme reductionism. Its advocates, who were seldom scientists, held that all crop growth could be interpreted in purely chemical terms, so that agriculture should be seen as a branch of chemical engineering, albeit a sophisticated branch. Pests and weeds, those living organisms that compete with the farmer for his land or its produce, could and should be regulated chemically. In a word, they should be poisoned and so annihilated. The opponents of this view held that natural, biological processes could be comprehended, if at all, only by means of a holistic approach. They felt the feeding of plants by inorganic mineral salts was somehow unnatural, that delicate ecological balances within the soil might be disturbed, that in the long run agriculture itself would suffer probably by a diminution in soil fertility and that the nutritional quality of food grown in this way would be impaired. They argued that the use of pesticides has so many side effects, most of which are unpredictable, that the disadvantages of using them outweigh the advantages. Chemicals, in fact, became equated with mortal sin and their use was essentially immoral.

Obviously, all these views are absurd and the arguments pretending to support them too weak to be taken seriously. They are precisely what Hegel might have predicted, however, and he would then have gone on to predict what would happen next. From the battle between thesis and antithesis there will emerge a synthesis: an approximation to the truth that borrows from both sides of the argument but in so doing adds something more. Today the old organic versus inorganic argument sounds sterile: the synthesis is emerging. In time, according to this dialectical theory, it will become the new thesis and the process will begin again at a new level.

For the moment, though, compromises are being made on both sides. For many years the organic school performed an essential service and once its arguments are stripped of their more extreme emotionalisms they make sense. The argument over chemicals must be considered separately from that over the mechanisation of agriculture, for although those who object to one sometimes object to both, this is not always the case and as the term 'organic farming' is most generally used, it implies nothing to do with mechanisation. Many organic farms are as highly mechanised as conventional farms and, indeed, organic farmers sometimes complain that machines have not been developed more specifically to meet their needs.

Let us begin with chemicals, then. As we have seen, a green plant is composed of carbon, hydrogen and oxygen which it obtains from air and water, and of a range of other elements that are supplied from the soil. In nature, these elements are recycled constantly. When anything dies or excretes, a material substance is deposited on or in the soil where it provides food for a hierarchy of organisms which attack it in waves, each group extracting the nutrients it needs from whatever material has been left by the preceding wave. In time the substance disappears, having been distributed among the saprophytic population and, of course, its predators. When these organisms die or excrete the process is repeated until eventually the original elements (apart from much of the carbon, which is oxidised to carbon dioxide and released into the air by respiration) enter the aqueous soil solution as simple ions. Thus, they are taken up again by a new generation of plants, passed to animals, and the great cycle continues.

There are losses. An animal may carry the substances it eats, and of which it is composed, to a new site. This happens, for example, each time a cat catches a mouse and takes it home. The elements that compose the mouse are lost to the system of which it was part. Some salts are carried out of the soil by 'leaching'. A few, such as ammonia, are lost by evaporation. These nutrients must be replaced by the weathering of rocks beneath the soil, by inflowing water, by animal transport, and by lightning. The underlying rocks are under constant attack from acids that drain down from the soil and enter into chemical reactions with the minerals of which they are composed. Rocks are also subject to bacterial attack. Very slowly, little by little, the chemical nutrients they contain are fed into the biological system. Water that leaches nutrients out of an area also leaches nutrients into it. They may not be the same nutrients, of course, or in the same amounts. This depends on the drainage pattern and on the location of the site within a watershed. The cat that carries the mouse home deprives one area of that mouse but supplies it to another area. Birds that fly long distances drop food and excrement to enrich the land over which they pass. Lightning supplies very large amounts of electrical energy that fix some atmospheric nitrogen by combining it with the oxygen and hydrogen in air and water. Some of this dissolves and falls in rain as a dilute nitrogen fertiliser.

Immediately, then, we must dispose of one organic myth. Plants take up nutrients from the soil solution in a simple chemical form. These nutrients are precisely the same as those supplied industrially as fertilisers. The difference between organic and inorganic farming relates to the way the nutrients are supplied; and not to the nutrients themselves. In this sense all farming is 'chemical'.

As we saw earlier, farming breaks the natural cycle of elements by removing nutrients far more rapidly than they can be replaced naturally. Unless nutrients are returned to compensate, it is likely that the nutrient status, and thus the fertility of the land will fall. This is not inevitable, for there are situations in which crop yields have been sustained over long periods without returning any nutrients and with no obvious reduction in fertility. This is pro-bably due to a locally rapid rate of natural replenishment; but it does not offer a satisfactory method of farming since the yields produced in this way are usually very low.

We have not conceded the argument to the chemists because although we must accept the need to supply nutrients, there is more than one way to do this. If you picture the entire process as a cycle, then it is possible to accelerate the cycle during the growth phase or during the decomposing phase. Organic farmers describe this as 'feeding the crop' or 'feeding the soil'. Conventional fertilisers feed the crop. The technique is simple, convenient, and susceptible to precise manipulation so that, at least in theory, precisely measured applications are made precisely where and when they are required. The alternative involves the acceleration of the process of decomposition. If organic matter is supplied in a partly decayed form but under circumstances that favour its rapid assimilation

109

into the soil, the purpose will have been served. Chemists have tended to misunderstand this approach, regarding such organic materials as no more than an alternative to chemical fertilisers. Thus, they have analysed composts and manures, found them to contain concentrations of nutrients much lower than those in industrial fertilisers, and so condemned them. The difference in nutrient concentrations is hardly surprising, since fertilisers are intended to supply pure nutrients in the most compact form that can be devised. What they measure, however, are 'available' nutrients, the nutrients present in a form that corresponds to crop needs. Suppose, though, that the organic material contains a rich soil fauna together with its food supply. Mix this with existing soil and an accelerated decomposition may ensue that releases a continual supply of nutrients. That decomposition can be accelerated simply is demonstrated by the fact that a pile of farmyard manure, or an ordinary (but well-made) garden compost heap will heat, due to the energy released by the biological and chemical activity within it. The advantages of this approach are that a broad spectrum of nutrients are supplied that may maintain or enhance the overall fertility of the soil, the slow rate of nutrient release reduces losses by leaching, the organic enrichment of the soil improves its structure, and organic materials are cheap. The disadvantage is that the process is imprecise and releases nutrients that may not be those required by a particular crop at rates that may be inadequate at some times and excessive at others.

The two approaches are not mutually exclusive and in practice most farmers use both. Fertilisers stimulate crop growth and this increased productivity also increases the amount of crop residues and plant and animal waste that can be returned as manure.

The largest single expense on a big arable farm is for chemicals and if the fertiliser bill can be reduced this is valuable. Organic materials are bulky, of course, and so more difficult to handle, but this problem can be exaggerated. It does not have to be handled by human muscle power: a manure spreader and one or two standard front-loading attachments for a tractor are sufficient to supplement standard cultivating implements. Nor does the organic material need to be applied to each field every year.

Usually it is applied, in liberal amounts, once or twice in the course of a rotation that may extend over six or more years. So despite its greater bulk, it does not follow that operating costs on organic farms are increased.

The organic farmer does not use conventional pesticides either (some pesticides derived from natural products are permitted) and if the use of fertilisers is mortal sin, the use of pesticides lies on the further side of anathema. Pests, weeds and diseases are controlled by the choice of disease resistant crop varieties where possible, and by good husbandry. Thorough and timely cultivations will kill annual weeds at the emergent stage so that over a number of years they cease to be a problem. Perennial weeds are more difficult and one of the main criticisms of organic methods is that it offers inadequate control of the more persistent weeds. There is no simple answer. It depends very much on local conditions. Determined cultivations will drive out most weeds eventually, but it may also cause them to spread as anyone who has tried to kill couch grass or docks by hacking at their roots will have discovered. Each piece of root grows a new plant. It should be said, though, that most farmers who have changed from conventional to organic methods found that weed problems did not increase to any great extent; some even found that weeds became fewer and easier to control.

By growing disease-resistant varieties and working to a well-planned rotation, farmers can avoid the worst of crop diseases. What they cannot prevent is the infection of their crop by wind-borne fungal spores. This can lead to much heart-searching as the farmer tries to decide whether he should sacrifice his principles and forfeit his organic status by spraying, or retain his integrity and lose his crop. In many cases the difficulty resolves itself because the crop is inaccessible to the sprayer.

Insect pests present a rather similar situation, a similar choice, and often a similar difficulty in applying any solution at all.

Does it work? The first interesting observation is that on most organic farms the pest, weed and disease problems are nowhere near so severe as conventional spraying programmes suggest they should be. This seems to imply that in conventional agriculture pesticides are used more frequently and in much larger amounts than can be justified. It does not imply that they should not be used at all, however, but only that better ways are needed to diagnose actual need and tailor the remedy to it.

The second observation is that if we are to consider organic farming as it is practised today we must forget the past. It is not enough to point out that farming was practised for rather a long time before chemical aids were introduced, because for most of that time it produced yields that would not be acceptable today. Nor must we imagine that because they dispense with one aspect of modern farming, organic farmers therefore dispense with all the innovations that have been introduced in modern times. They are neither practising, nor trying to recreate, some archaic farming system. They complain that virtually all the research and development funds devoted to agriculture at least since about 1945, have been invested in an agriculture assumed to use chemical aids. Were similar funds devoted to the search for particular composting techniques to deal with particular materials and to supply composts for particular crops, for example, the results might be very profitable indeed. They would like to see more efficient ways of reclaiming and using urban organic wastes including sewage and they would welcome more subtle methods of pest control.

There has been one classic study of the economics of organic farming conducted in the mid-1970s among farmers in the US corn belt by the Center for the Biology of Natural Systems at the Washington University in St Louis, Missouri. It found that while organic farmers produced yields that were rather lower than those of farmers growing similar crops on similar soils and under similar conditions, but using chemicals, their yields were sustained more easily during years when the weather was bad. The overall effect was that in years of good or average weather they made slightly less profit per acre than conventional farmers, but when the weather was bad their profit was slightly greater. The conclusions are important. They mean that it is possible to farm economically without using modern chemicals. Later extensions of this early study investigated the experience organic farmers had of the change from conventional to organic methods. It had been widely accepted that this would involve an immediate drop in yields as fertilisers were abandoned, followed by a gradual increase as the fertility of the soil recovered under the new regime. The study found that many of the farmers noticed no great difference in their profits during the change.

The organic farmers in the study used about one-third of the energy used by the conventional farmers. There has been much discussion in recent years of the energy demand of food production, based on studies made in the USA and in Britain.

If you cultivate your vegetable garden by hand and use no chemicals or machines to help you, it is possible to calculate the amount of energy you expend in working from the food you eat and the known food energy requirements of a human body. This energy input can be compared with the output of the garden, also measured in food energy terms, so that your energy efficiency can be expressed as an input to output ratio. The average figure for allotments in the UK is $1:1.3$. This is to say, they produce 1.3 units of energy for each unit of energy they expend. If industrial chemicals or machines are used, the same procedure can be used, because energy is just energy, no matter how it is derived. With machines and chemicals yields will rise but so will the energy expenditure, because this is now being supplemented by energy derived from fossil fuels burned in the manufacture and operation of the aids that you use. So if, say, you grow carrots using fertilisers, pesticides and a tractor, you will produce only 1.1 units of energy for each unit you expend. There is not much difference. When you grow brussels sprouts, though, whose nitrogen requirement is higher and whose yield is lower, you will produce only 0.19 units of food energy for each unit of energy you expend, and when you grow winter lettuce in a heated greenhouse you will produce about 0.002 units of energy for each unit you expend. Similar budgets have been calculated for most farm enterprises and they suggest that it may be possible to improve the efficiency with which energy is used in food production. This is the main reason why studies of organic farming are worthwhile. If you would like to know more about these energy budgets, including an account of how they are made, you should read *Energy and Food Production* by Gerald Leach, published by and obtainable from the International Institute for Environment and Development (see p. 188 for the address).

(see p. 188 for the address)

What implications do these findings have for the use of machinery? Farm machines are very expensive. This fact alone may alter their energy requirement by making it necessary for them to last longer, so that the energy cost of their manufacture can be spread over a larger number of years. That would amount to an increase in the efficiency of energy use. They may have to reduce their operating costs by using cheaper fuels, using them more thriftily, or both. This, too, would amount to an increase in their efficiency. Apart from this, it is difficult to imagine an appropriate kind of modern agriculture that did not use machines. If the alternative is to use draught animals, in most instances this amounts to a loss rather than a gain: animals require land to feed them that otherwise could be feeding humans. You might say that in this respect machines were being used to gain land, and most of us might agree that the bargain is a good one.

Apart from arguments about their energy efficiency and general design, most of the objections to the use of machines are trivial. It is true that their weight compacts the soil, but by deep ploughing every few years pans can be broken quite easily. The vision of computerised farms may sound absurd and aesthetically displeasing, but already it is possible for a tractor to be operated by remote control, and accidents with tractors account for more deaths and serious injuries on farms than anything else. While no one really believes that the day will come when all farm operations are mechanised, if for no other reason than that this would not be sensible socially in times of high structural unemployment in manufacturing industries, computers and remote sensors might be used to considerable advantage. The charge that the man sitting on his tractor is less observant than the man walking on the ground is true. It is also true that modern mechanised farming treats average situations only, while in practice conditions may vary quite widely from one part of a field to another part of the same field. This problem might be overcome by means of sensors deployed at different parts of each field to feed certain information (on soil pH, temperature, moisture, etc) to a computer that would process it to give early warning of changing conditions that required special treatment. Computer technology is environmentally benign, modest in its requirement for raw materials and it uses little energy, either in manufacture or in use. Its social effects are more problematical, but there seems to be no reason why organic farmers should not accept it.

You must reach your own conclusion. If you would like to know more about the theory and practice of organic methods, the principal organisations promoting them in Britain are the Henry Doubleday Research Association and The Soil Association (see p. 188 and 189 for the addresses). Information on organic farming in other countries is collected by the International Institute of Biological Husbandry (see p. 188 for the address).

In years to come it is likely that computers will be used to assist farmers and that machines will become more advanced and more efficient. The old organic-inorganic argument is resolving itself in an Hegelian synthesis. New ways are being sought to supply nitrogen to crops without incurring the costs of industrial fixation. Pest control is becoming more subtle. People and their governments are becoming concerned about the impact of modern farming on the environment and on the appearance of the landscape. So things are changing. For the time being, though, it may be best to treat the organic farmers with some respect. In the past they have made extravagant claims, but many of their arguments are sound and where their actual results have been checked they have proved not miraculous, but nevertheless impressive.

7 The enterprises

Provided the climate and soil are suitable, it is possible to practise most kinds of agriculture even on the smallest holding. The limitations are not physical, but economic. Let us suppose that you have ten acres of land that are capable of growing any kind of produce. If you grow wheat, you may expect a yield of about 2 tons per acre, or 20 tons from the entire holding. In September 1978 the best milling wheat, suitable for bread, was selling for about £84 a ton, so your income would be £1,680, against which you would have to set the cost of production, which we will discuss later. Let us suppose that instead of wheat you decided to grow maincrop potatoes. These were selling at about £25 a ton. However, the average yield for potatoes is about 10 tons per acre, so your total output would be 100 tons of potatoes, worth £2,500, and your production costs would not be much different. If you were to grow cooking apples, say, Bramley's Seedlings, at the height of the season they might sell to the wholesaler for about 14p per pound or £314 per ton. The average yield for cooking apples is about 4 tons per acre, so the total output would be about 40 tons, worth something like £12,500. Suppose that instead of producing plant crops you built up a very small dairy herd. On 10 acres of land you might stock, say, five milkers. They might yield about 1,000 gallons a year each, so your annual output would be about 5,000 gallons. At September 1978 prices milk was selling for about 43p per gallon, so your income for the year would be about £2,150.

It is clear, therefore, that on a small scale the commodities we have considered can be ranged in order of increasing profitability as wheat, milk, potatoes and, the winner by several lengths, apples. This means that cereal production can be made profitable only on rather large farms, while dairying can be profitable on smaller farms. But even 10 acres is too small for dairying, and vegetable and fruit production is the most obvious commercial enterprise for the smallholder who wishes to provide a living for the family.

Horticulture and orchards

Clearly, then, if a small area of land is to be managed profitably, either it must yield some crop very heavily, or produce something with a high market value; or, ideally, it should do both.

Horticultural crops are valuable. Traditionally, they were grown only close to large urban areas which provided the markets. Today, however, good transport systems have eliminated this need. There are relatively few, very remote, areas that are beyond the economic reach of the marketing and distribution network.

So horticulture is a viable proposition in most places. However, now that this fact is well known, so horticulture has become intensely competitive. Vegetables and fruit suffer from the major disadvantage of being seasonal, because they do not store well without processing, and the processing they require necessitates fixed plant that is not available to the small-scale grower. Thus, fresh produce is vulnerable to glutting, and a consequent large drop in price. There are two possible solutions to these problems. The first is to grow an unusual crop that other horticulturalists do not grow. The second is to arrange for your crop to be ready before that of your rivals. There may be a third choice, in the form of contract growing, but we will consider this in a later chapter on marketing.

There are exotic crops that are profitable, but in most cases they are exotic for the good reason that either they are troublesome to grow, or the yield is poor. Courgettes, for example, retail at a high price. If you have plenty of space for them, they can be an economic proposition. However, the plants require a large area to produce a rather small number of product; and courgettes are unpleasant to cut because the plant possesses many minute, sharp prickles that can inflict painful cuts. Also the crop must be cut at frequent intervals because unless they are cut at just the right moment, courgettes continue to grow and soon become too large

117

for the market. So few growers bother with courgettes, and the price for them remains high. Aubergines, too, sell for a high price, but in Britain they can be grown only under heated glass, which makes them a costly enterprise. The same argument holds for capsicums.

Most growers forget about the unusual crops (which therefore remain unusual!) and seek to race their competitors to the market, while at the same time seeking to extend the cropping season. This is done by growing many crops under glass.

The crops that are grown outdoors are those that occupy much space, are not especially valuable, and are hardy in the British climate. They include potatoes, conventional root vegetables such as turnips, swedes, carrots and parsnips, legumes such as beans and peas, onions, and brassicas. All of these crops are also grown on a farm scale in fields. Glasshouses are reserved for less hardy crops such as lettuce, cucumbers, strawberries and tomatoes, which cannot be grown commercially outdoors in our climate. Flowers are also grown under glass in most cases, as a conventional horticultural crop. The tomato is a curious tropical plant that does not require high temperatures because its natural habitat is the high slopes of the Andes. Being tropical, however, it can afford to set its fruit late in the year and is sensitive to changes in the length of the day, beginning to form fruit only when the days are shortening This has advantages in regions where the winter is invariably mild; but in northern Europe it means that the fruit may fail to ripen because the temperature falls too low before the process is completed. Amateur gardeners can grow tomatoes in the open successfully in good years, but the commercial grower cannot afford to risk the bad years, and his crop must be protected from fluctuating changes in temperature.

Glasshouses

Glasshouses these days are made from various plastics as well as from glass. A suitable material must give good light penetration, good thermal insulation, and good durability. Late in 1978, the most common materials cost about £11.29 per square yard (£13.50

per sq m) for glass; £13.88 (£16.60) for polycarbonate; and £19.56 (£23.40) for acrylic. Glass is the traditional material as it allows excellent penetration by short-wave radiation (but not long-wave), but it breaks easily, and heat is lost through it readily. Polycarbonate and acrylic materials offer better thermal insulation so that in a heated house constructed from these materials fuel bills could be up to £2.40 per square yard lower than with glass; because they are lighter they require less framework than glass (often about 50 per cent less) thus enabling more light to enter. The most common difficulty with plastics is that they degrade under ultraviolet light so that although they are stronger than glass they still need replacing every few years. Some growers accept this need for periodical replacement and use heavy-duty polythene sheeting mounted on semi-circular hoops to make houses that are deliberately temporary. Plastic materials are being improved all the time and many can be used in double thicknesses to improve insulation without reducing light penetration significantly. A house glazed with acrylic, for example, may reduce heating bills by 45 per cent. There are many variations, and before buying the newcomer should consult *The Grower*, which is the principal trade paper for the horticultural industry.

It is better to build new glasshouses than to buy old ones because the rise in energy costs in the early 1970s has stimulated great interest in energy conservation, for which new houses are more likely to be designed. This applies not only to the materials from which the house is constructed, but also to its shape as well. Trials at the Ministry of Agriculture, Fisheries and Food Experimental Horticulture Station, Efford, Hampshire, have shown that considerable savings can be made by the use of thermal screens. These are flexible sheets of thermal insulating material (several different materials have been tried) that are drawn, like curtains, at night. They greatly reduce the loss of heat by long-wave radiation and by convection to the skin of the greenhouse and conduction through it. However, it is not always easy to fit them to older houses, which have an inconvenient roof shape.

Heating is of obvious importance, and although all commercial glasshouses are not heated, most are. Again, the cost of installing the equipment varies widely and the cost of operating it depends much less on the temperature the grower wishes to maintain than on the efficiency of his insulation. It is possible, especially in a new greenhouse, to use the ground on which the house stands as a heat store, either by sinking heavily insulated walls deep into the ground all around the house, or by burying an insulating material in the soil itself. The traditional way of doing this was to bury bottles or jam jars upside down and empty, with their tops lying just below the root area of the crops. Rather large numbers of bottles or jars are needed, since they must touch one another throughout the house, and they should be more or less the same size. The system is still a good one, and its efficiency can be increased by filling the glassware with an insulating substance such as glass fibre, polystyrene chips, urea formaldehyde or polyurethane foam. Any of these will convert the ground into a heat store that warms during the day and releases its accumulated heat at night, so helping to maintain a steady temperature.

Most heating is supplied by the burning of oil, natural gas, or some other fuel. A gas-fired system, new, may cost from about £350 upwards, when installed. Solar heating can be used, but there are disadvantages in that it supplies heat most efficiently in summer, when heating may not be needed at all, and solar collectors mounted on the roof reduce light penetration. Heat pumps may also be used. These use a small electric circulating pump and compressor to move a fluid between the inside and outside of the house to extract heat from the outside air and release it inside. Efficient heat pumps suitable for glasshouses should be on the market within the next few years. You can be kept informed of developments by the Natural Energy Association (see p. 189 for the address) which monitors such matters, but any dramatic developments are certain to be reported in the trade Press.

If the ground on which the glasshouse stands is insulated, does this not remove the soil, either directly by doing just that, or indirectly by altering its depth or temperature? The answer is that a warm soil is likely to be beneficial to crop growth; but even if the soil is lost in this way it may be no bad thing. In the unnatural conditions of a glasshouse, soil can be a nuisance.

What happens is that in providing optimum conditions for the growth of his crop plants, the grower also provides optimum conditions for the development of pests and diseases. Not only do parasitic organisms thrive, but the high cost of space in a glasshouse compels the grower to pack plants together so that each house will contain a large number of identical plants, all at the same stage of development. This amounts to a virtually inexhaustible supply of food for parasites and non-human herbivores. As the years pass, so their populations increase until eventually the soil becomes so infested that further cropping is impossible.

The solution to the problem is to sterilize the soil in each glasshouse every year. Sterilization usually lasts for about 12 months. It is done by pumping hot steam through the soil and, predictably, this is expensive and can cost £50 a house or more. The alternative is to dispense with soil entirely, and much glasshouse produce today is not grown in soil.

It can be grown in an inert material, such as peat, either in troughs or in 'grow bags'. The sterilized peat is used merely as a physical support for the plant and as a medium for the retention of the water and nutrient that are added to it. The medium must neither dehydrate easily nor become waterlogged. After it has grown two or three crops, the peat is thrown away by spreading it on the ground outside. Any disease it carries will not affect the quite different outdoor crops and the disease and pest organisms will not survive long in the open.

The next stage beyond soil-less peat culture, which is a form of hydroponics, is to dispense with the peat as well, and move to a fully hydroponic system. The nutrient film technique (NFT) is one of the latest and most attractive versions of hydroponics and it has caused great excitement among growers. Shallow channels run the length of the glasshouse, slightly inclined so that a nutrient solution fed into them from a header pipe flows slowly down them to form a thin film of nutrient solution. The channels are covered with a substance having slits or holes through which seedlings are planted. They are held in position by the cover, and as their roots react to the nutrient they spread and give added support. Surplus nutrient solution is collected in a gutter at the lower end and returned to the reservoir and header pipe by means of a circulating pump. NFT offers many advantages, not least of which is its simplicity: an NFT system could be built by any competent handyman from plastic guttering and piping, and nutrient mixtures can be bought to use in it. The NFT system is not in wide commercial use as yet, partly because it is still new and partly because it is still being adapted and developed for growing certain crops. It does bring crop diseases under control, weeds are no problem; but there are still pests, though, and they are a much more serious problem in glasshouses than they are in the open. Further information about it can be obtained from ADAS or from the Glasshouse Crops Research Institute (see p. 188 for the address) which invented it.

A glasshouse contains a large number of genetically identical plants, all at the same stage of development. Should a nucleus population of pests manage to enter the house, they can multiply freely. When their population becomes so large that, in nature, they would migrate to find a new source of food, the glasshouse prevents them from doing so, and once the pest has become established in the house it becomes very difficult indeed to eliminate it. If conventional pesticides are used, high kills may be obtained, but among the insects there will be individuals that are naturally immune to the poison which will live. These will multiply so that in time a population emerges that is resistant to the pesticide and, possibly, to a range of similar pesticides. Pesticide resistance develops in this way in the open, and houseflies, for example, are now quite resistant to DDT; but in a glasshouse the process is much accelerated. The only satisfactory solution is to use some method of biological control, usually based on the use of a natural predator of the pest. Biological control techniques have been developed for a number of pests and details of them are obtainable from the Glasshouse Crops Research Institute and from ADAS. Prevention being better than cure, it is important to design the glasshouse in such a way as to increase the obstacles in the path of any migrating insect, and to reduce the risk of infestation by disease organisms as well as insect pests. Human visitors should be kept to a minimum and workers should be careful at all times and most especially when moving from one house to another.

Glasshouse crops must be supplied with water by irrigation and because the cost of water to the grower is now high, every effort must be made to avoid losses. The type of irrigation will depend to some extent on the crops being grown, but many systems now deliver water below the surface of the growing medium to reduce losses by surface evaporation.

Mineral nutrients can be supplied in various ways, but as we saw earlier it is possible for crops to suffer from light saturation. The rate of photosynthesis can be increased in some cases by providing carbon dioxide and equipment and pumps for this purpose are on the market. Since carbon dioxide is the principal by-product of the combustion of fossil fuels, however, it may not be necessary to instal equipment to enrich the atmosphere with carbon dioxide if the house is being heated with a fossil fuel heater. It is worth remembering, though, that the heater may not be in use during the summer, when carbon dioxide may be needed most.

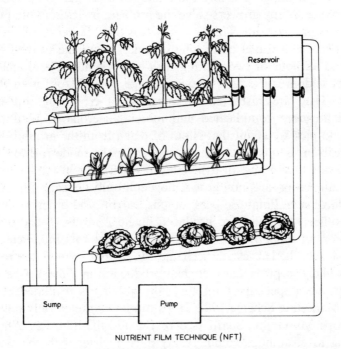

NUTRIENT FILM TECHNIQUE (NFT)

Outdoor growing

Other equipment for horticulture is simpler and cheaper than its agricultural equivalent. While a small tractor is useful, the place of the plough, harrow and weeders may be taken by the rotavator, which is perfectly satisfactory for a small area. Outdoor irrigation is needed during dry periods.

Soft fruit other than strawberries is usually grown outdoors and, in general, it calls for less labour than annual vegetable crops. Apart from insects, which attack some fruit bushes, the main pests are birds. These are best discouraged by means of netting, erected on a rigid frame around the entire crop as a 'fruit cage' large enough for people to enter and work.

Orchard crops require work only at certain times of year. If pruning of those trees that require it is performed regularly, correctly, and at the right time, it is not a laborious or onerous task.

The major expense facing the fruit-grower is that of harvesting the produce. Many growers solve the problem by inviting the public to pick their own fruit. This system seems to work very well indeed, and people will travel quite long distances from the nearest town to spend an hour or two picking fruit at weekends. These amateur pickers seldom cause any serious damage, to the crop or to themselves. They are restricted to low-growing crops, of course. It would be more complicated and more dangerous to permit the public to pick tree fruit that is out of reach from the ground. Even this problem is being solved, though, since the modern dwarf and semi-dwarf trees bring all their fruit to within easy reach.

Certain crops are not grown horticulturally, except for small-scale local sale. Potatoes, peas, onions, carrots and other roots and some other vegetables are produced on huge farms specialising in them, or on other farms as part of a normal rotation. Peas, for example, can be harvested mechanically, so that farm-scale production is likely to prove cheaper than production in a market garden.

Hops are a specialist crop, and hop growing is regulated by the Hops Marketing Scheme 1932. Hops can be marketed only through the Hops Marketing Board (see p. 188 for the address). Anyone wishing to grow hops commercially must register with the Board.

Potato growing is also regulated and anyone wishing to grow an acre of potatoes or more (0.4ha) of which any are to be sold must register with the Potato Marketing Board (see p. 189 for the address).

The growing of apples and pears, other than cider apples or perry pears, is controlled by the Apple and Pear Development Council (see p. 187 for the address) and anyone who wishes to plant 5 acres (2ha) or more with 50 or more trees must register with the Council.

Arable cropping

Arable crops, as opposed to horticultural crops, include the cereals (wheat, barley, oats, rye and mixed corn) and crops grown on a field scale for human or livestock consumption, such as potatoes, peas, various beans, sugar beet, maize and various roots.

Arable farming is subject to some climatic and topographical limitations. Wheat suitable for bread-making can be grown safely only in the eastern countries of England in an area defined by a line drawn in a roughly south-westerly direction through the centre of Co. Durham, then almost due south to meet the south coast to the east of the Isle of Wight. However, for reasons we discussed earlier, the smallholder is unlikely to try growing wheat for sale—although you might like to grow a little for your own use. Cereals intended for feeding livestock can be grown in a much larger area, but even then there are difficulties in western districts because the moist climate makes ripening uncertain.

All arable farming calls for orthodox farming equipment. A tractor is essential, and two are advisable to allow for inevitable breakdowns and servicing and to give greater flexibility. There are many farm tasks that can be performed in all weathers, and they must be interrupted when the weather permits essential field operations. If the routine task used the tractor and some of its ancillary equipment, valuable time can be lost in removing this equipment and attaching other implements.

In addition to the plough, a harrow or several different harrows, and cultivator are required, as well as equipment for distributing

Wheat in Britain for the 1980s

126

fertiliser, manure and seed. Rollers are advisable on some land. Manure is spread by a flail-type spreader in which the contents of a trailer are moved towards the rear by an endless belt or auger and thrown out by rotating flails, or by a rotary spreader in which flails made from lengths of chain rotate on a longitudinal axis to throw the material from a container in the shape of an open-topped cylinder. The rotary spreader can handle semi-liquid manure, it pulverises material more completely, and it achieves a more even spread. Where livestock is housed on concrete without the use of straw bedding, and in dairies that must be hosed down frequently, the manure is collected in pits in liquid form, as a slurry. This can be spread by means of a pump connected by hose in fields adjacent to the slurry pit, or by mobile tanker in fields further away. Granular fertilisers are spread by a distributor in which the fertiliser is fed from a hopper to a spinning disc. The same machine can be used to broadcast seed. Seed drills, however, deposit seeds in straight rows at fixed distances apart in all directions, and so they are much more efficient and require smaller amounts of seed to ensure the establishment of a good crop stand. Potatoes are planted mechanically by a more elaborate machine that cuts a drill into which it drops seed potatoes fed automatically from a hopper or by hand into cups arranged around the circumference of a wheel.

The cost of all this equipment varies widely. It is often possible to pick up serviceable but obsolete machines at low prices. These are good value provided it is still possible to obtain spare parts for them. A good secondhand seed drill might cost about £1,500. A slurry tanker might cost roughly the same. A fertiliser distributor might cost about £800, and a harrow anything from about £250. A potato planter costs rather more.

Harvesting equipment is even more expensive. Cereals and crops other than roots can be gathered with a combine harvester, which will cost anything from about £7,000 secondhand, and potato and sugar beet harvesting equipment costs £3,000 or more.

Once the crop has been harvested, it must be stored and in many cases this calls for special conditions. Grain will deteriorate unless it is stored dry, and this may necessitate drying equipment which can be very expensive indeed. Potatoes must be dry on the outside,

127

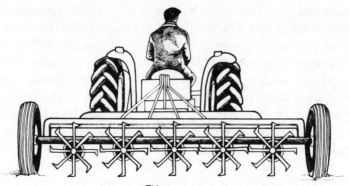

Thinner

Manure spreader

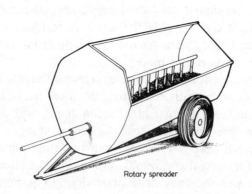

Rotary spreader

Pallet
fork

Shovel

Manure
fork

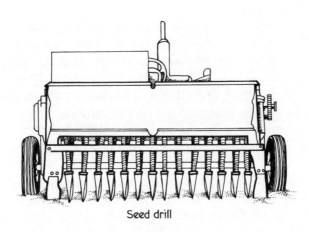

Seed drill

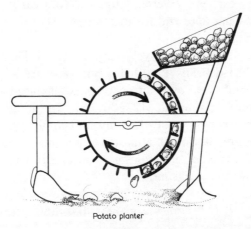

Potato planter

but must not be exposed to the light. Sugar beet is not stored, but carried straight from the field to the processing factory.

The buildings required for arable enterprises need not be elaborate. Obviously, the crop must be stored in bins in a dry, cool place. If the farm grows cereals but keeps no livestock to utilise the straw, then the straw will be sold off the farm. If it is sold quickly, it will require no storage more complex than a dry floor and a weatherproof covering. If it is to be used on the farm, it must be stored in a dry barn. Machinery should be kept under cover when it is not in use.

Fertiliser requirements for arable crops vary according to the crop, the soil and the weather. Cereals are grown as either a spring or a winter crop. The latter is sown late in the year, emerges before the winter sets in hard, then resumes its growth early in the following year. It produces an earlier and heavier crop than one sown in the spring and so wherever the climate permits, farmers prefer to grow winter cereals. In the north of England and over much of Scotland, it is possible to grow spring cereals only. Winter cereals require more fertiliser than spring cereals. For winter cereals the average amounts used per acre are about 57 units N, 44P and 40K (57:44:40) for oats; 74:44:41 for barley; and 78:45:41 for wheat. For spring cereals the equivalent figures are 50:33:31 for oats; 60:33:34 for barley; and 58:35:35 for wheat.

Potatoes require much more, maincrop varieties using rather more than earlies. Average figures for early potatoes are 127:136:154 per acre and for maincrops 141:148:196. Sugar beet uses 118:78:146.

Vegetables also use relatively large amounts. Peas receive about 23:39:46; broad beans 17:39:40. But these are legumes that can obtain much of their own nitrogen. Brassicas need heavy feeding, cabbages receiving about 122:86:164. In addition to buying fertiliser, the farmer must also buy and apply pesticides, though the amounts are very much a matter of personal choice, and despite the blandishments of the salesmen many farmers prefer not to spray as a routine measure.

When the cost of buildings, machinery, seeds and chemicals are added together, it becomes apparent that arable farming is costly and difficult to make profitable on a small area.

This does not mean, however, that the smallholder cannot grow arable crops. It may not be possible to sell grains at a profit, but it can be cheaper to grow them on the farm for feeding to livestock than it is to import them. So many stock farms grow small amounts of cereals and fodder crops for internal use.

The cost of doing this can be much lower than the cost of large-scale arable farming. By cropping a small area, the amount of work involved is reduced and although timing remains critical, older, smaller, slower equipment is often adequate. If it is not, the work can be contracted out and much farming is performed by agricultural contractors, most commonly where the scale of operation does not warrant heavy investment in machinery. The main disadvantage is that the contractor will be in demand to perform the same operation, using the same equipment, on many farms simultaneously, so that the timing of each operation may be less than perfect.

We usually think of arable farming as a means for producing the obvious end products of grains and other plants, but there may be a few alternatives, which we will consider in the next chapter.

Grass

Humans cannot digest grass and so we tend to undervalue its role in agriculture. This criticism is directed not simply at townfolk. Farmers, too, have devoted much less attention to grass than it warrants, at least until very recent times. In fact, grass is as important an agricultural crop as any other plant as it provides the base for the ruminant livestock industries.

While most of Britain, apart from the highly mineralised soils of the uplands, can grow good grass, there are many areas that can grow nothing else. These areas occur, broadly speaking, on the western side of the country, in most of Scotland, and on the Downs.

Grassland can be sorted into three categories: rough grazing, permanent pasture, and temporary pasture or 'leys'.

Rough grazing accounts for a little over 16 million acres in the UK, 11 million of them in Scotland. This is about one-third of all agricultural land. It is the poorest land, found in the mountains of

Scotland, the Cumbrian fells, in the Pennines and Cheviots, the Welsh mountains, and on the high moors of the south west of England. The soil is commonly shallow, sometimes with rocks outcropping, and the land is often steep, rocky or otherwise impossible to cultivate. Plant growth is often inhibited by the cool, wet climate as well as by the soil. Indeed, the two are related closely, since a benign climate that encourages plant growth thereby builds up a rich soil composed of the remains of earlier plants.

Most of the rough grazing land cannot be cultivated, but in places it is being improved. If machines can get on to it and if there is a sufficient depth of soil, the land can be ploughed up to improve drainage and sown with 'pioneer' crops that can withstand the harsh conditions. Later the land can be ploughed again and seeded with better grasses, so converting it from rough grazing into leys.

Unimproved rough grazing is used for feeding livestock which are often stocked at very low densities, sometimes with as little as one sheep to 10 acres or one cow to 50 acres. The pasture is too poor to sustain dairying and animals being raised for meat are usually sold off for fattening on better pastures elsewhere. It is not possible to conserve grass for winter feeding or to grow other fodder crops for winter keep. The principal crops are wool and live animals.

Rough grazing is seldom farmed by itself. Farms usually consist of some better land, known in Scotland as 'in-bye' land, and rights to common hill grazing. It is possible, therefore, for a smallholding to have access to a much larger area of grazing land that can be used during the summer. As we saw earlier, this is the customary practice in crofting. It is reckoned that to provide a reasonable living for a family, the farm should be large enough to support about 400 breeding ewes and some breeding cattle.

Permanent pasture means just what its name suggests. It is grassland that has been grazed, sometimes for centuries, with no other kind of management. Constant grazing prevents the area from reverting to scrub and eventually to forest, but it may not prevent the invasion of the sward by more aggressive and less nutritious species of grasses and herbs, so that the quality of the pasture may decline. Permanent pasture, in the sense of grassland that has not been ploughed for five years or longer, occupies about 12 million acres in the UK. It can be improved by fertiliser treatment, the average application rate being about 86:42:31 per acre; but the recommended treatment for most permanent pasture is to plough it up and reseed. This would convert it into a ley, or temporary pasture, lasting from 1 to 5 years, and such leys occupy about 5 million acres in the UK, an area that has remained fairly constant for a number of years. The reason ley farming is not more popular is most probably associated with the general lack of awareness of the importance and potential of grassland. Why should a farmer go to the trouble and expense of ploughing his fields and sowing grass when they grow grass already?

The reason is very simple. The output of the farm can increase dramatically. Indeed, it is safe to say that no smallholder who wishes to raise cattle or sheep can afford the luxury of permanent pasture. The only difference between grass and any other plant crop should be that once sown, the grass may remain in place for more than one year.

Leys are often part of an arable rotation. If grass seed is sown together with a cereal crop ('undersown'), it will grow more slowly than the aggressive cereal and by the time the cereal crop is harvested the grass will be established securely and much time will have been saved.

Traditionally, pastures consisted of many species of grasses and herbs, including many legumes to provide nitrogen. Today, a ley may consist of no more than two grass species and legumes may be omitted because a fairly heavy use of fertiliser produces more rapid and lusher growth. The average use of fertiliser on temporary grassland is about 91:57:41 per acre in the first year, and 122:45:38 in each subsequent year. Most grassland would benefit from twice this amount of nitrogen and some would benefit from still more.

Grass is seldom irrigated in Britain, but over much of the country it would benefit from irrigation during the driest weather. There is much evidence to suggest that pastures suffer from water stress to an extent that reduces their productivity significantly.

133

Having said all of this, it is necessary to make some qualifications. In some parts of the country the permanent pasture is of good quality. It might be improved by adding fertiliser, manure or lime but, if it were ploughed, the topsoil might be buried too deep to benefit the new seed, or too shallow to kill out the old grasses. Temporary pasture, on the other hand, is inherently less stable. Because it is composed of simpler mixtures it may be less able to withstand invasion from wild grasses, so that it is unlikely to develop into worthwhile permanent pasture if it is left. It must be regarded as a crop quite different from permanent pasture.

One of the many paradoxes in agriculture is that while plants cease to grow during the winter, animals continue to eat. So the land that feeds them for one part of the year must also supply them with food for the remaining months. Grass must be grown for conservation as well as for immediate grazing. Theoretically, the simplest way to provide winter keep might be to set aside some of the grassland for winter use. In practice, this is seldom possible. Since grass that is grazed in winter will not regenerate until the spring, a large area would be required, making this an uneconomical use of land. If the land becomes wet in winter, the weight of the cattle on it may damage both the grass and the structure of the soil, reducing it to churned mud. The process is called 'poaching' and people try to prevent their children from playing on garden lawns in winter for the same reason.

It is also an uneconomic use of grass. As the grass grows very tall and ripens, its stems become tough and woody and its nutritional value falls. After it has released its seeds it will die to form a mat of dead and useless grass that inhibits the growth of new grass beneath it. Even if this does not happen, sheep are nibblers and cannot graze in long grass. They suffer badly if they are kept on very wet ground, which encourages foot rot in most breeds. Cattle can eat long grass, but if they eat grass that is very long it will take them longer to chew it so that they actually eat less than they would if the grass were shorter. Since the grass itself is of inferior quality, in many cases they could not obtain sufficient to sustain them, let alone enough to produce milk or to gain weight. Cattle have very regular habits and they will spend just so many hours a day grazing (usually 8) and no more, because they need the additional time to chew the cud and digest it. If the food is of poor quality, they will not spend longer eating to compensate.

The solution, then, is to conserve grass. Traditionally, this was done by making hay. Today hay is giving way to silage, haylage and to dried grass. The important difference relates to the amount of nutritional value that is lost by each method. Haymaking may result in losses of up to 35 per cent of the nutritional value of the grass, silage loses up to 25 per cent, haylage loses up to 20 per cent, and dried grass loses about 5 per cent. Why, then, is hay-making still the most common method used?

The answer is familiarity and, to a lesser extent, cost. Hay-making is simple, its techniques are well known and the equipment required for it is relatively cheap. Silage making is rather more expensive and complicated, with a greater possibility of failure, and grass drying is more expensive still.

To make hay, the grass is cut at the peak of its quality and dried in the field, being turned ('tedded') regularly to ensure thorough and even drying. Then it is baled and stored. It must be handled with care, for in its dry form it is brittle and easily damaged, and it must not be stored wet; but no great skill or investment are needed. A secondhand mower might cost about £400, and a baler about £750 to £1,000. Any dry barn will do for storage, although the traditional method was to store hay in thatched ricks in the open.

To make silage, the grass is also cut at the peak of its quality, but in addition to the mower that cuts it a chopper and blower are needed to cut the grass into small pieces and feed them into a trailer. This attachment might cost about £500. The grass must now be stored in a special container where it can be packed tight. The container may be a silo, costing £1,000 or more, or a clamp consisting of nothing more than walls on a concrete floor. The walls themselves can be bought in prefabricated sections 6 to 10 ft. high. The grass is fed into the container, packed down, and covered with some form of weatherproofing. In this airless condition, bacteria commence the decomposition of the grass, but in doing so they convert some of the sugars into lactic acid, which kills other micro-organisms and prevents the decomposition from proceeding beyond a certain point. The aim, therefore, is to accelerate the formation of acid; for this purpose, molasses can be added as a cheap, readily available sugar, as well as various proprietary additives. However, if too much acid is formed the silage will be unpalatable to stock and if too little is formed decomposition will go too far and the grass will turn into something rather like garden compost. So a simple mistake could cost the farmer his winter feed and while inferior hay is still of some use to stock, failed silage is not.

Whether hay or silage is made, the water content of the grass is important. Well-made hay contains about 30 per cent moisture. Silage is made directly from fresh grass, but if it still contains its original 80 per cent or more of water, then as it settles in the clamp and begins to ferment it will release surplus water as a highly noxious liquor. To avoid this, grass is often chopped twice and allowed to wilt for 24 hours before ensiling. The risk of causing serious and illegal pollution of surface water is a further drawback to making silage.

Grass drying is simpler. Freshly cut grass is dried rapidly by a hot air blower. The dried grass can then be pressed into convenient cubes for feeding. Nutrient losses are small and there is not much to go wrong. The trouble arises from the cost of installing and operating the drying equipment. Most farmers cannot afford it. It might be possible, though, to adapt grain-drying equipment for this purpose and for the farmer wishing to dry grass to hire the grain drier on the farm of his cereal growing neighbour. At least this would reduce the capital cost. Of course, it is not much help if the grower of grass is in Devon and the cereal farmer is in Suffolk, but in some regions such an arrangement might be feasible.

Haylage is somewhere between silage and hay, as its name suggests. The grass is cut and left to lie in the field, as with haymaking. When it has a moisture content of about 45 per cent and is still easy to handle, it is baled, taken to a barn, and dried with a hot air blower. A blower suitable for this task might cost £500 or so, but a cheaper fan can be run from a tractor power take-off.

The number of animals that can be fed from an acre of grass-

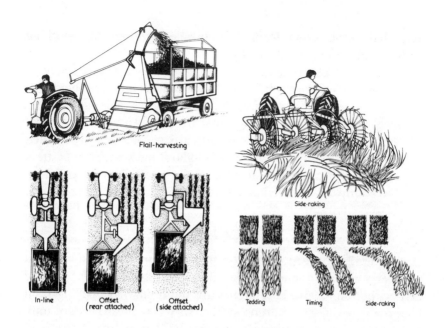

Flail-harvesting

Side-raking

In-line Offset (rear attached) Offset (side attached)

Tedding Timing Side-raking

land depends, obviously, on the quality of the grass. It also depends, rather less obviously, on the efficiency with which the grass is used. You may imagine that there is little anyone can do to persuade a cow or sheep to eat more efficiently, but this is very far from true. A cow, grazing for its precise 8 hours a day, will seek out and eat first those grasses that appeal most. The less palatable grasses will be left and in time they may come to dominate the pasture so that although the pasture may look good, from the cow's point of view it is deteriorating. The solution to this is to control the grazing by confining the animals in temporary fences or hurdles. Only cattle and lowland sheep can be confined in this way. The fences are arranged to divide the field into paddocks or strips, depending on the size and shape of the field. As each area is finished the animals are moved to the next and the grass they have left uneaten is mown to remove any advantage to the less palatable species. By the time the animals return to the first area the grass will have grown again, largely because it was manured heavily during the first period of grazing on it. On good pasture it is possible to stock about one cow or five sheep to an

137

acre, but using some form of controlled grazing the stocking density can be increased greatly.

The term 'stocking density' does not refer to the area occupied by the animals at any one time. As a glance into any field will confirm, a herd or flock grazing in a 10 acre field achieve an absurdly high stocking density if that were the way it is measured. It refers, rather, to the area of land that is needed to provide each animal with all the food it needs throughout the year, so that grass being grown for conservation, or land sown to winter keep, grains or forage crops, is counted as well as the land that is being grazed.

Cattle

If you decide to keep cattle, the first decision you must make is whether you will produce beef or milk, or both. It sounds a simple matter, but dairy and beef breeds are quite different, having been bred for very different purposes. The dairy cow must produce milk from grass and concentrate feedingstuffs. The more of the food she eats that is converted into milk the better, so there is no advantage in having a large animal. An animal that converts her food into fat or muscle on her own body is useless. If she does this, then perhaps she should be regarded as a beef animal. The beef animal must convert as much as possible of its feed into meat, but the cows of beef breeds produce no more milk than is needed for their own calves.

Historically, then, beef and dairy breeds have been developed along different lines and one cannot substitute one for the other. It is true that there have been all-purpose breeds. The South Devon, popular today in the south west of England, is one such animal, and it is descended from a breed, now extinct, that was a three-purpose animal, being used as a draught beast as well as a producer of both milk and meat. In modern terms this is not very efficient as higher yields can be obtained from more specialised stock.

The modern compromise is to use beef bulls to serve dairy cows so that the calves can be fattened for beef, having inherited the good beefing qualities of their sires. As the British dairy herd has

138

become dominated by the Friesian–Holstein and as the beef herd has been dominated by the Hereford, it is not surprising that many of the calves you see are black and white with white faces. They are Hereford x Friesian crosses, raised for beef off the dairy herd.

To some extent the decision makes itself, for dairying is impracticable except on the best pastures and even then concentrates are needed to supplement the diet. A modern dairy cow, designed to produce 1,000 gallons or more of milk every year, is a milk-producing machine, a product of advanced technology, and she must be fed accordingly. That milk must be made from something! In the same way, the beef animal must be fed well if it is to fatten quickly, but here the diet is not quite so critical since a slower rate of growth can be tolerated. Beef can be produced on poorer land.

As dairying is the more costly enterprise, requiring milking equipment and a dairy that conforms to the Milk and Dairies (General) Regulations 1959, it is hardly worth considering commercial dairying with a herd of less than about 20 milkers. Beef cattle have no special requirements, so they may be easier and more profitable on a small acreage.

Next, which breed to buy? Again, this decision may settle itself, because you will buy your animals—at any rate to start with— from local markets, and so you will have no choice but to buy the breeds that are in local use. The most popular dairy animal is the Friesian–Holstein. It yields very large amounts of milk, but requires much rich feeding. The Ayrshire produces rather less milk, but is content with correspondingly less food. Ayrshires are advertised regularly in the trade Press, but they may not be obtainable at ordinary markets in all parts of the country. The simpler alternative to a large Friesian is a Channel Islands animal, a Guernsey or Jersey. These are smaller animals and their milk yield is lower, but, being smaller, they eat less and so can be stocked at rather higher densities; they are also efficient converters, producing a milk with a high butterfat content that at present attracts a quality premium. This situation may change in the next few years because of concern about the effects on health of high dietary intakes of animal fats. A Guernsey or Jersey makes an admirable house cow.

The Hereford or Hereford x Friesian is the most common beef animal, but the small, all black Aberdeen Angus has the advantage of fattening well on grass. In fact, these animals do not make good meat if they are fed a highly concentrated diet. The Hereford x Friesian, and most other modern crosses, on the other hand, are adapted to intensive or semi-intensive systems and diets much enriched with protein.

These are only a few of the choices, however, and the small-holder, or indeed anyone seeking to raise animals only on grass, and especially in poorer areas or harsher climates, might do well to consider one of the older breeds that used to produce well under precisely these conditions. There are many such breeds and the best source of information about them is the Rare Breeds Survival Trust (see p. 189 for the address). In order to familiarise yourself with these breeds, the best book on them is *The Chance to Survive* by Lawrence Alderson, published by Cameron and Tayleur in association with David and Charles.

In most areas cattle must be kept under cover during the winter if they are to develop at a satisfactory rate or continue to produce milk. It may also be necessary to keep them out of fields where there is a risk of poaching. In any case, since grass does not grow during the winter there is little food for them outdoors. Their accommodation need not be elaborate: a yard made from concrete that drains well, covered with a roof, makes a covered yard. Animals may be penned within the yard, pens costing about £15 to £20 each and made from tubular metal. A fashionable alter-native form of accommodation is the individual cubicle for each cow, or the 'cow kennel'. These can be constructed by the farmer either from scratch or by using one of the DIY kits that are obtainable.

Unless you are prepared to wash the yard daily and have a large slurry pit to collect the mixture of water, urine and faeces that will drain from the yard, straw should be supplied for bedding. The cattle stand on the straw and as it becomes soiled more straw is added on top. At the end of the winter, when the cattle return to the pastures, the mixed straw, urine and faeces will have become farmyard manure, dry enough to lift with a manure fork attachment to the front of a tractor, and a useful (organic farmers might say, essential) source of nutrients and soil conditioning for arable crops or new grass.

In addition to winter quarters, dairy cattle must have a dairy. This is not essential if all you have is one dairy cow but if you are milking commercially, you must have a building in which it is possible to maintain high standards of hygiene.

While they are being milked, cows must be tethered or otherwise prevented from moving, and they must be fed, partly to distract them and partly as a means of rationing their food. A convenient way to arrange this is provided by a pen with a gate at both ends, the cow entering through one gate and leaving through the other. The cow does not have to back out of the pen and it is simple to keep the cows that have been milked separate from those that have not. Made from tubular metal, pens of this kind cost about £25 new.

Hand milking is almost unknown today. It is still possible, of course, but it is exhausting physically and if more than one or two animals are to be milked it is probably advisable to invest in a milking machine. These can be obtained in any size to suit the number of cows in the herd, and very small ones are made for one or two cows. There are several manufacturers of milking machines, the best-known being Alfa-Laval and Fullwood (see p. 187 for their addresses). After milking, the milk must be stored in a tank and chilled, and it must be kept stirred unless the cream is to be separated from it. Churns can be used for home consumption, but they are not acceptable to the Milk Marketing Board, who require milk to be pumped from a tank. A simple tank to hold 300 or more gallons can be obtained for under £30, but with all the ancillary equipment it requires, the price of a secondhand one may be closer to £500.

How do you choose a good animal? The simplest and most reliable method is to take along a friend who is experienced at judging cattle. If you are buying calves, you will need to know something of their known ancestry, which will give you some idea of the way they will develop later. Obviously, they should be healthy and clean, with strong, well-formed limbs. The hind

141

Brucellosis: Attested and Eradication areas as at 1 November 1978

142

quarters should be clean and well haired. If the calf appears to have diarrhoea, this may be due to nothing more serious than a change in its diet. On the other hand, it could indicate a serious intestinal infection. If the calf has no hair in this region this, too, may indicate scouring (diarrhoea). The navel should be clean and free from infection. If the calf is punched in the region of the navel it should not show pain. The animal should breathe easily, without coughing, and when it takes a full breath its ribs should be visible. If the calf is to become a milker, the bags should be the same size and the teats should be all more or less the same size and spaced evenly. If they are too close together or at markedly different heights, it may be difficult to attach the milking machine or for calves to suckle.

At late 1978 prices calves cost about £80 each. A cow ready to be milked costs about £400.

Cattle must be free from bovine tuberculosis; and brucellosis is being eradicated from the national herd. Tuberculosis testing is done at three-yearly intervals, or more frequently in areas such as south-west England, where TB is more common. Each animal is tested and those that react positively must be slaughtered, as must all cattle that are known to have been exposed to infection by contact. Compensation is paid for slaughtered animals, based on 75 per cent of their market value up to a limit that was increased in November, 1978, to £425.

The eradication of brucellosis is proceeding county by county. In counties that are declared free from the disease, all cattle are tested at intervals and those that have brucellosis are slaughtered, compensation being paid at 75 per cent of the market value up to the limit of £425. In areas where eradication is not complete, any farmer may apply to have his cattle tested. If after a series of tests, they are shown to be free from the disease, then the herd is accredited. In eradication areas, where eradication is compulsory, diseased animals are slaughtered, compensation being paid at the full market value up to the £425 limit, and a course of treatment is prescribed for the others. When this is completed the herd is tested again. Once animals are accredited they must not be brought into contact with none-accredited stock or they lose their accreditation.

The movement of livestock is regulated at all times and the farmer is required to keep a register of all movements of stock on and off the farm. In some cases it is necessary to obtain a permit before stock can be moved. Details of these requirements can be obtained from Divisional Offices of the Ministry of Agriculture, Fisheries and Food.

Cattle belonging to each registered farmer are identified by means of ear tags bearing the farmer's number.

Maintenance of the day-to-day health of cattle depends on correct feeding, hygiene in quarters in which they are confined for any length of time, and common sense, but if any animal appears unwell for reasons you do not understand, veterinary help must be obtained. Mastitis is probably the most common ailment of dairy cows. A sample of milk must be examined for signs of mastitis at each milking. The disease is kept to a minimum by correct drying off at the end of each lactation, and treatment is not difficult.

Information on many aspects of livestock farming with cattle is contained in a range of leaflets obtainable free from the Ministry (see p. 189 for the address). Information on dairying can be obtained from the Milk Marketing Board (see p. 189 for the address).

Sheep

As with all livestock, the main produce from sheep is more sheep. The rate of breeding is very critical. The lambing rate is calculated as the size of the flock after each breeding season, allowing for mortality among lambs and ewes, expressed as a percentage of the former size. Thus, a lambing rate of 150 means that after lambing the flock is half as large again as it was before lambing. The product of the enterprise consists of the surplus animals, sold as older ewes no longer required for breeding and lambs not taken into the breeding flock, which may or may not be grown on for sale as fat lambs ready for slaughter.

The environment imposes its own conditions on sheep enterprises. In the rough pastures of the mountains there is insufficient winter keep to maintain more than a breeding nucleus, so the lambs are not fattened. They are born in early spring, raised through the year

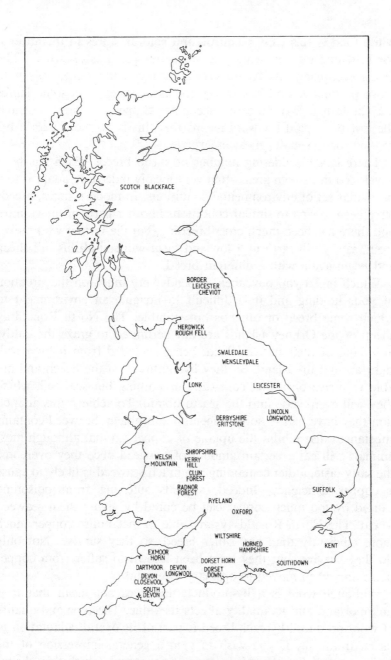

Origins of breeds of sheep

while food is relatively plentiful, and sold as stores in the autumn for fattening the following year on better pastures elsewhere. The farms occupying less harsh terrain do much the same, only with more productive and less hardy breeds of sheep, and some lambs may be fattened. In all cases, sheep are clipped for their wool, but the low price paid for wool means that this is no more than a by-product of the main, meat enterprise.

There is a bewildering number of sheep breeds. Each has been developed in its own area, often very locally indeed, to adapt it to a particular set of environmental conditions. In modern times, breeds have been moved to similar conditions in other parts of the country and there has been much cross-breeding, but the farmer who moves from, say, a hill farm to a lowland farm will sell all his hill sheep and begin again with a different breed.

Which breed you buy, then, depends very much on the situation of your holding and it is difficult to imagine an environment to which some breed or other is not suitable. The North Ronaldsay sheep of the Orkney Islands are not permitted to graze the cultivable land of their native island, being excluded from it by a wall right around the island. So they live entirely on the beach and are able to thrive on a diet consisting of nothing but seaweed, which they will even wade into the sea to obtain. To achieve this adaptation they have had to solve a metabolic problem. Seaweed contains substances that inhibit the uptake of copper, so that although most animals will eat a certain amount of seaweed once they overcome the salty taste, a diet containing too much seaweed is likely to cause a copper deficiency. Indeed, animals suffering from poisoning caused by too much copper can be cured by giving them seaweed to eat. The North Ronaldsays are able to metabolise copper much more efficiently than any other breed, so they survive. Not only do they survive, but they have been known to suffer from copper poisoning when moved to ordinary grassland.

Although wool is a by-product, this does not mean that it is unimportant, and its quality affects its value. The type and quality of wool produced by each breed is part of its overall adaptation to its environment. If you wish to gain a general impression of the most common breeds and the type of country in which they thrive,

146

read *British Sheep Breeds, Their Wool and Its Uses,* published by the British Wool Marketing Board (see p. 187 for the address). The book describes 36 popular breeds, but before you make a final decision it might be worth considering the possibility of building up a flock of one of the endangered breeds, described by Lawrence Alderson in his book *The Chance to Survive* (published by Cameron and Tayleur in association with David and Charles).

Many attempts have been made to intensify sheep production but this has proved very difficult. All sheep are very prone to parasitic infestation and disease, transmitted by contagion, and the problems are magnified when animals are confined in close proximity to one another. Modern research concentrates more on developing breeds that will produce triplets or quadruplets at lambing (rather than the customary singletons or twins) and that produce lambs which are large in proportion to the ewe, and lambs that grow quickly.

Despite the difficulties of keeping sheep intensively, it is common these days to overwinter sheep in covered yards in the harsher uplands. This greatly reduces mortality from injury or starvation. Mortality can be high in areas of heavy snowfall. Ewes are usually brought close to the farm at lambing time to provide them with better pasture and to make it easier to observe them and to render assistance where necessary. Often they are placed in individual pens, which make it very easy to give them all the attention they need. Most sheep mate in autumn, when the days are shortening, and lamb in spring, but there are breeds that lamb at any time of year.

Other than this, sheep need no accommodation.

Sheep must be dipped in a substance approved by the Ministry of Agriculture, Fisheries and Food to control parasites. Dipping for the control of sheep scab is compulsory, but it is possible for farmers to share the cost of constructing a dip.

Most people can learn to shear a sheep, but it *is* a skilled job and the novice must be taught by an expert as there is some risk of injuring the sheep and a much greater risk of damaging the fleece by not removing it correctly and in one piece. This, in turn, could reduce the value of the fleece.

Sheep can be fed entirely on grass. In the lowlands, in good pasture, stocking densities can be increased by controlled grazing, the sheep being folded across the land by means of movable fences or hurdles. Only the lowland breeds can be confined in this way, however. Hill sheep are accustomed to wide expanses of terrain and are used to covering large distances in search of their food. Thus, they regard walls, fences and hedges as obstacles to be overcome rather than as insurmountable barriers. The best hope of containing them is by using a high wall, a high, thick hedge, or an electric fence positioned at precisely the right height. Even if the sheep can be confined, they may not thrive under such conditions.

Even in the poor hill pastures it is important to ensure that the herbage is grazed efficiently. Sheep nibble short grasses. Overgrazing, with sheep or cattle, damages the land and may destroy the pasture. Undergrazing is only marginally less serious, especially for sheep. Mats of long, dead grass that suppress new growth effectively sterilise the pasture so far as sheep are concerned.

Sheep can be stocked together with cattle. Since the grazing habits of the two species are different they do not compete for food while they are grazing; so where both are kept the total stocking density will be rather higher than it would be if stocking rates for the two were calculated separately. Neither do they suffer from the same parasites. For example, if cattle graze first, sheep that follow will nibble at the relatively short grass left by the cattle but will not pick up any bovine parasites.

AI is not available for sheep, so a ram is required for breeding. It is not worth keeping a ram for very small flocks, so arrangements must be made to borrow one at mating time. In hill farming areas and in some other areas as well, it is an offence to allow rams and uncastrated ram lambs to roam at large on unenclosed land during certain periods of the year; and at other times the only male animals allowed to wander free are those approved as satisfactory for breeding purposes by the Ministry of Agriculture, Fisheries and Food. This regulation is designed to prevent random breeding and to ensure that breed lines can be kept pure and breeds improved.

Routine measures designed to maintain flock health include dipping and inspection of hooves for signs of foot rot, and general observation to detect unusual behaviour. There are many diseases and ailments caused by parasites. Most can be treated quite easily, but early treatment is advisable and if the condition is not to be communicated to the rest of the flock, any suspect animals must be kept isolated until they have been given a clean bill of health.

Apart from disease-carrying organisms, the most serious enemy of the sheep is the dog. Dogs hunt sheep naturally. This characteristic is exploited in the training of sheepdogs, so that they can behave aggressively towards sheep but in a controlled manner. Retired sheepdogs should be kept away from sheep for they may revert to their natural behaviour, and the most mild-mannered pet dog is potentially dangerous. Farmers are permitted to shoot and kill any dog on their land that is wandering unchecked and which they suspect may harrass sheep.

Lambs cost about £40 to £50 each, so depradations by stray dogs must be taken seriously.

Pigs

The pig is a non-ruminant animal, which means that although pigs will eat a certain amount of grass and other cellulosic material, they cannot metabolise either in the manner of cattle and sheep which have complex stomachs, or in the manner of horses, which push large quantities of herbage through their gut fast and obtain as much nutrient as they can. In fact, pigs will eat anything that humans will eat, but they are less fastidious.

Traditionally, pigs were kept on farms as scavengers. They ate wastes such as kitchen scraps, potatoes that were unfit for human consumption, stale bread, and such grain as could be spared for them. The system was much more efficient than it sounds. Wastes that were otherwise useless were converted into high-quality protein and fat presented in a very palatable form, and surplus grain was stored. In years when the grain harvest was good there was plenty of food for pigs, so people ate bread and the number of pigs increased. When the grain harvest was poor and there was less bread to eat, the pigs were reduced in number. During the 1950s and 60s, the world as a whole had very large surpluses of grains, so feeding stuffs for pigs were cheap. The pigs began to eat nothing but grains and their numbers increased to such a level that entirely new systems of management were devised to cope with them. Thus was born intensive indoor pig production, and breeds were developed to thrive under the conditions it imposed.

So, just as the farmer planning to keep cattle must choose whether to specialise in beef or dairying, the pig farmer must also decide whether he will embark on intensive production or extensive, mainly outdoor production. If he decides to embark on an intensive system, his capital costs will be high. He must have a farrowing house, in which the piglets are born, and a fattening house in which the weaned piglets ('weaners') are penned in groups according to their age and size. If the pig farmer decides to fatten them for pork or bacon (bacon animals should be larger than porkers), he must calculate what this will cost in feed and what he is likely to earn from their sale. He will probably find that the enterprise can be made economic only if it achieves a very high throughput, with large numbers of animals being brought to market weight as quickly as possible. He must prevent food losses by controlling the temperature in the house, so that food energy is not expended in maintaining a constant body temperature. He must use precisely the correct feed in precisely measured amounts. He must watch for signs of illness that could develop rapidly into an epidemic and decimate his herd.

If he decides that he cannot afford a pig unit large enough to provide him with an income, his alternative is to sell weaners to a specialist who will finish them. This requires less capital investment (one house may be saved) and, of course, feed costs are reduced.

The intensive pig farm need not occupy a large area of land, since it reckons to import all its feed. In other words, it buys the produce of the land that actually feeds the stock.

This raises complex questions of the future of world grain prices and some people believe that now the world grain surpluses are gone, grain prices will remain high—at least for the remainder of this century—so that intensive pigmeat production will become an increasingly costly enterprise. As it is, feedgrain prices have

150

trebled since about 1970. Increases in feed costs cannot be passed on to the eventual consumer because pigmeat must sell in competition with beef and lamb. If its price rises, people will buy less. So the profitability of pig farming is in doubt and in recognition of these difficulties, which are likely to be long term and structural rather than temporary, pig production is not encouraged by support in the way that cattle and sheep production are.

This does not mean that pigs will vanish from the landscape nor does it suggest that the smallholder should avoid pigs. Indeed, the smallholding may be the place where pigs flourish in years to come because it is possible to produce pigmeat more slowly but much more cheaply on a small scale.

Apart from their meat, pigs produce manure that is richer in nutrient than manure from cattle or sheep. This means it is more noxious should it escape into rivers, but it also means that pigs provide the best means of enhancing the fertility of land quickly and cheaply.

Pigs can still be fed on waste foods and modest amounts of grain. They need not be housed in costly intensive units and if they are not, their accommodation can be quite simple.

There are two methods suitable for a small-scale enterprise. In the first, the pigs are kept in the open all the time. They must have shelter at night and from the worst of the weather, and this can be provided by arks, which are no more than small huts, semi-circular or triangular in cross section, placed in line with the prevailing wind and closed at the upwind end. The pigs are confined by means of a temporary fence. They will eat whatever food they can find and when they have exhausted the surface of the land they will begin to dig for roots. In fact, they can provide a very elementary form of cultivation and will remove many troublesome weeds and dung the land at the same time. When they have gone far enough they are moved to new ground, their old paddock is cultivated, and sown to an arable crop.

Alternatively, they can be kept in sties. A pig sty is a simple structure. At the rear it must provide shelter and an area for dunging. Pigs will always excrete in one place. At the front it must provide a small yard surrounded by a wall high enough to prevent the larger pigs from escaping (about 4ft) and the trough from which the pigs feed.

These low cost systems will take longer to produce finished animals than more intensive systems, but they require very little capital investment and provided feed can be supplied cheaply they can be profitable. The meat they produce can be of high quality.

The unit may produce animals to market weight and the beginner is well advised not to attempt to breed pigs, but to buy in weaners and fatten them. Having gained experience in this way it is possible to select from the weaners one or two females that can be kept as breeding sows. They must be healthy, strong, and have well-formed, well-spaced teats. AI is available for pigs in some areas, but elsewhere it is necessary to find a farmer with a boar and to take the sow to him. Once a breeding regime has begun, it is possible to raise some animals for meat and to sell others as weaners.

The rise of the intensive pig industry has reduced the number of pig breeds and a very limited selection of breeds is available at most markets. These have been proved to be the most prolific animals, however, and the ones that grow most rapidly to produce good-quality meat. However, you may wish to consider the possibility of raising an older breed, possibly for a specialist market. Information about such breeds can be obtained from the Rare Breeds Survival Trust (see p. 189 for the address).

Pig accommodation must be kept clean and washed out thoroughly after each batch of animals has left for market. If waste foods are used, these must be made into a swill, by boiling them in water for not less than one hour. This is a legal requirement, and if you feed pigs on waste foods commercially you must prepare the food in special premises, with a 'dirty' and 'clean' area. The purpose of this treatment is to prevent the recycling of disease organisms.

Pigs are vulnerable to foot-and-mouth disease, as are all hooved animals, and they are also susceptible to swine vesicular disease which is almost indistinguishable from it symptomatically. Both are controlled by slaughtering all animals that may have been exposed to infection.

The movement of pigs is controlled and must be recorded in a movements register; further, a licence to move animals off the farm must be obtained from the Ministry of Agriculture, Fisheries and Food.

Poultry

Like pigs, poultry are non-ruminants and they will eat anything that humans will eat. Traditionally, they have been used in the same way as pigs—as scavengers and converters of wastes into eggs and meat. The development of intensive battery and broiler systems has occurred in parallel with the similar developments in the pig industry and for the same reasons, with the small difference that since about 1970 feed prices have increased for poultry by slightly more than they have for pigs.

There are other differences, though. The poultry industry became dominated by a small number of producers with flocks measured in tens of thousands, so that it is almost impossible for the small producer to compete. This means that intensive poultry production at present is, to say the least, a dubious investment.

There remains a market for free-range eggs and meat, however, and the small producer can supply this. Even so, it is doubtful whether the enterprise can do much more than cover its costs. Free-range poultry can be kept in a run, or it can be folded over grassland. Folding is the better method provided the grass can be spared for the purpose, and poultry manure encourages rapid and lush growth.

The capital investment is small. Houses are needed, and a standard poultry house, about 12ft long by 6ft wide by 6ft high will accommodate 20 or more birds. The house is mounted on small wheels and is towed to a new position in the field at regular intervals. It is surrounded by a wire mesh fence to confine the flock to a small paddock. Under this system it is possible to stock poultry at up to 120 birds per acre provided they are not grazing with other stock. If they are, a stocking rate of about 50 birds per acre is more appropriate. The birds will eat some grass and herbs, as well as any small invertebrate animals they can find, and this diet is supplemented by grains and/or waste foods, prepared as a mash in the same way that pig swill is prepared, but to a drier consistency. The birds must have a supply of fresh water to drink.

The difference between this method and the run is only that in the run the flock is not moved. This means the house can accommodate rather fewer birds, the overall stocking rate is lower, and care must be taken to ensure a reasonable standard of hygiene. The house can be bought quite cheaply, or built by any competent amateur carpenter, and a house in a run does not need wheels.

Whichever method is used, predators must be excluded. Foxes are the most notorious hunters of domestic poultry, but mink and other members of the weasel family can also cause great damage and, of course, they can enter through a much smaller opening. Buzzards and other large birds of prey have been known to take small birds, and cats will kill young chicks, but will not attack full grown hens. If the flock is to breed its own replacements, eggs can be collected and incubated in a warm place, or broody hens can be allowed to hatch their own clutches of eggs. Young chicks must be provided with their own accommodation until they are large enough to look after themselves, mainly to protect them from predators. If they have been hatched by a hen, their own mother will take good care of them, but she will not fight off marauders on their behalf.

There are many breeds of poultry from which to choose and each has its own devotees. Probably, the most common bird is the Rhode Island/Light Sussex cross, which lays well and has an added advantage: its chicks are white if they are male, and brown if they are female. This makes the sexing of them very easy as soon as they develop feathers. Marans lay small numbers of eggs with very dark-brown shells, which are popular.

Hens are prone to a number of diseases, but there are many excellent books for the small scale poultryman that describe their symptoms and treatment. One of the best, which also describes many breeds and pays close attention to diet and productivity, is *Poultry Culture for Profit* by Rev. T. W. Sturges, published by Spur Publications.

8 Moneyspinners

The smallholder suffers many economic disadvantages because of his inability to benefit from economies of scale, but these apply only to the more conventional kinds of enterprise. Where enterprises require little space, then the smallholder, too, can operate on a relatively large scale. What is more, these are often enterprises that are beyond the scope of the conventional farmer because they do not combine well with orthodox farming. Many of them can be used to satisfy small, specialist markets where returns may be high. Once you begin to think of what might be possible, the list grows at an almost exponential rate. What follows, then, is no more than a very rough-and-ready guide to some of the more obvious ideas. Because there are so many and because each one is separate from the others, the suggestions are arranged in alphabetical order.

Bees

There is a constant demand for honey and the retail price is always high. Compared with other enterprises, beekeeping requires little capital investment. Considering late 1978 prices, £150 would be sufficient to equip the beginner with a new hive, stock and necessary equipment and protective clothing. Secondhand equipment is cheaper. More than one hive would be needed for commercial production, but it is advisable to begin with one and to acquire more hives later. For one thing it is essential to discover whether you or any member of your household is allergic to bee stings. If you are, then a sting that would be no more than a trifling annoyance to most people may be very dangerous indeed, and you should not attempt to keep bees.

Honey is only one of the products and, commercially, it is not the most important. Beeswax can be sold for making high-quality candles and polishes, and also to suppliers of beekeeping equipment for making wax foundations. Wax production is more reliable than honey production, so for many beekeepers the sale of wax provides the basic income to which the sale of honey adds a welcome supplement. Honey can also be made into mead and other drinks. A licence from HM Customs and Excise is necessary if you plan to make alcoholic drinks for sale.

Apart from its profit potential, beekeeping has the further advantage of requiring no more space than that on which the hives stand and a small open space in front of each hive to permit the bees easy access.

Unfortunately, there are also disadvantages. It is possible to have too many hives in a particular area, so that the flowering plants provide too little nectar to supply all the bees. Before commencing, it is as well to find out whether your district is over-populated with bees already, or whether it is likely to become so in the foreseeable future.

Only certain plants are suitable 'bee plants' for producing honey. If these do not grow in your area, then beekeeping may be impracticable. Clover and heather are good bee plants and these are quite common, and fruit orchards depend on insect pollination, but it is best to make sure. A district with few bee plants will become overpopulated with bees more easily than one with many.

Honey production is not reliable. A hive may produce 60lb of honey in a year, or none. It may even have a negative productivity if there is insufficient nectar even to feed the bees themselves, so that you have to provide food for them.

Beekeeping is fascinating, but it must be learned, by reading and by instruction from experienced beekeepers. There are many excellent books on beekeeping and the Ministry of Agriculture, Fisheries and Food publishes a range of pamphlets and leaflets on the subject. Advisory Leaflet 283 *Advice to Intending Beekeepers* is free from the Ministry's Publications Division (see p. 189 for the address), and Bulletin 9 *Beekeeping* can be purchased from HMSO. An excellent, inexpensive introduction to the subject is *Home Honey Production* by W. B. Bielby (EP Publishing Ltd).

The organisation that advises and assists beekeepers is the British Beekeepers Association (see p. 187 for the address). The Association will put you in touch with your own county association, which will give you access to much expert advice and assistance, as well as informing you of the best and most competitive suppliers of equipment and stock. It may be possible to purchase secondhand equipment through the Association.

Dairy Produce

While it may not be economic to sell very small amounts of milk, it may be profitable to process the milk into clotted cream, cream cheese, soft cheese, hard cheese or yoghourt, for sale through specialist outlets such as health food shops. In places where farmhouse cheeses are still made on the premises, demand for them usually exceeds the supply.

There are several books on cheese-making and other dairy processing, and the Ministry of Agriculture, Fisheries and Food issues free leaflets on *Cream Cheese* (Advisory Leaflet 222), *Clotted Cream* (Advisory Leaflet 438), and *Soft Cheese* (Advisory Leaflet 458).

The by-products of milk processing, skimmed milk or whey, can be used to feed pigs.

Fish Farming

Most of the trout sold in freezer centres and supermarkets has been produced on farms. The trout has been domesticated for at least a hundred years, but until recently most farmed trout were sold for restocking rivers for anglers. This still provides a useful outlet, but today the fish can be sold for direct human consumption, and it is only when this is done that the enterprise qualifies as 'agricultural' for the purpose of grants. The fish used are different. The trout that is raised for human consumption is the rainbow, originally introduced from North America, which grows more rapidly than the native brown or sea trout.

Only a small area of land is needed, but it must have access to fresh or sea water. The inflowing water must be clean and well oxygenated. You will need to construct tanks or ponds and preferably these should be capable of being drained completely. Ideally, they should be under cover, which makes it easier to control water temperatures and to deter predators. If they are built in the open, they must be protected with a cover of wire mesh, for example, to keep away fish-eating birds such as herons.

The capital cost need not be high provided the site is suitable. An initial investment of about £650 will provide and instal a small tank, all its necessary ancillary equipment, and a base load of fish to deliver an eventual full annual production of 240 to 720lb of fish. An investment of about £4,000 will provide a much larger installation, with an eventual annual output of 1 to $1\frac{1}{2}$ tons of fish.

Permissions are required from planning authorities and from the water authority, to which all fresh water belongs.

Although trout are the fish farmed most commonly, where suitable salt water sites are available the farming of marine fish is possible. Research into this, using plaice, sole, turbot, bass and other species has resolved most of the problems and full-scale commercial application only awaits the day when it becomes cheaper to cultivate fish than it is to hunt wild ones.

Salmon are being farmed experimentally in Scotland and in France, and, again, the problems of the full life cycle have been resolved. Freshwater coarse fish were farmed in the Middle Ages but lost popularity when better transport services and refrigeration began to bring fresh marine fish to urban markets, the marine species proving to have a more popular flavour. Today coarse fish can be farmed for restocking rivers and it is possible that some may sell in specialist, high-price markets. Carp, for example, might prove popular in Asian restaurants, and pike might find outlets in European gourmet restaurants. Most of the fish we eat are carnivorous species; and this position in their ecosystems limits their productivity. The carps are herbivorous, however, and their productivity is much higher.

Marine shellfish, especially oysters and mussels, are not difficult to culture either for human consumption or, in the case of mussels, to provide feed for other fish. Lobsters can be 'ranched' by breeding them in captivity and releasing the juveniles to be caught in pots later, and the farming of scallops (coquilles St Jacques) is also possible on the basis of developmental work done in France and Britain. The market for scallops is huge, especially in France, and prices are always high.

There are many books on fish farming. Useful information can be obtained from one of the leading suppliers of equipment, Field, Stream and Covert (England) Ltd (see p. 188 for the address).

Flax

The rise in the interest in handspinning provides a small market for flax fibre for spinning and weaving into linen. Flax is grown as a field crop and it must not be grown on the same ground more than once in every seven years or so, because its nutrient demand is high and it returns nothing, all parts of the plant being used. It is no more difficult to grow from linseed than any other field crop, but it requires extensive processing to extract the fibre. Using a modern variety and fairly heavy fertiliser applications it should be possible to obtain rather more than 1.5 tons of fibre from an acre of land. The plants are pulled from the ground, not cut which would damage the fibre, then dried and 'rippled' to remove seed heads. The stems are 'retted' by soaking them in still water to commence the decomposition of the outer bark; dried to arrest the retting process before it reaches the fibre; and the stems are 'scutched' or shattered mechanically. The flax is then 'hackled' to comb the fibre free from the bark. The process is described briefly by Ailsa Allaby in *The Survival Handbook*, by Michael Allaby, Marika Hanbury-Tenison, John Seymour and Hugh Sharman, published in hardback by Macmillan and in paperback by Pan; while the growing of flax is outlined in *Home Farm* by Michael Allaby and Colin Tudge, published in hardback by Macmillan and in paperback by Sphere.

Game

People are willing to pay high prices for the right to hunt or fish on private land, and areas not suitable for cropping can be managed to provide good habitat for birds that are reared in captivity and released. Pheasants are the birds most commonly used for this purpose. They are not especially difficult to breed and rear in pens and they are released gradually into their prepared habitat to allow them time to learn to find their own food. They remain fairly tame throughout their lives, so that their reaction to humans is to approach to be fed rather than to flee from them. Thus, apparently wild birds can be shot rather easily to give the hunter a feeling of skill and achievement. The ethics are dubious, but the profit is considerable.

If you own riparian rights on a stretch of a salmon or trout river, fishing rights can be sold at apparently absurdly high prices. The prices are not quite so absurd as they seem, since a skilled angler should be able to catch sufficient fish to cover his or her costs.

Garlic

It sounds absurd, but with garlic retailing at 10p a bulb or more, a garlic farm could be very profitable indeed. The crop is not difficult to grow from cloves in southern England, provided planting is timed accurately. Growing from seed is much more difficult and unreliable. The crop requires much weeding, but little attention otherwise. Once harvested and dried, it keeps well, so that it can be marketed over a period of time long enough to avoid the risk of glutting.

Goats

Dairy goats can be stocked at a higher density than cattle. Contrary to many old music-hall jokes, goats do not thrive on a diet of garbage and tin cans. They prefer tough, fibrous vegetable matter to grass, and many breeds prefer not to eat grass at all. In addition, they require some concentrate feedingstuffs if they are to provide much milk. They are not especially hardy in the British climate, and must have accommodation to shelter them at night and in bad weather. Usually, this accommodation takes the form of kennels just like dog kennels only larger.

Their lactation is longer than that of cows and a good milker can give up to a gallon a day. Goat milk does not suit everyone's taste, but provided the goat is fed properly the milk will not be tainted. Cow's milk also taints easily if the animal is not fed correctly. The problem and its avoidance are described in *Taints in Milk* (Advisory Leaflet 322), published by the Ministry of Agriculture, Fisheries and Food.

Unlike cow's milk, goat's milk can be deep-frozen and it is said to be helpful to some asthma sufferers. Also, people who are allergic to cow's milk can usually take goat's milk.

Dairy goats are not subject to the Milk and Dairies (General) Regulations 1959 (which apply specifically to cattle), so that while they should be milked under hygienic conditions there are no special legal requirements. Goats are usually hand-milked. They are susceptible to a range of diseases, as are all animals, but they are seldom ill if they are cared for properly.

The Ministry of Agriculture, Fisheries and Food publishes a free leaflet on *Dairy Goat Keeping* (Advisory Leaflet 118) and there are several popular books on the subject. One of the best is *Goat Husbandry* by David Mckenzie, published by Faber and Faber. Further literature, advice, and details of suppliers of stock, can be obtained from the British Goat Society (see p. 187 for the address).

Herbs

There is a large demand for culinary herbs, a rather smaller demand for medicinal herbs, and a tiny but growing demand for dye plants. Because most herbs are attractive plants, a herb garden is likely to attract visitors, so that unless it is designed specifically for drying herbs on a large scale, a main source of income for herb gardens and nurseries comes from the sale of plants. Herbs can be grown on very small areas of quite poor or difficult land and many are perennials that require much less attention than any annual crop. A wide range can be grown because most of the plants themselves are small and crop relatively heavily, herbs being used in very small amounts.

Many flowering herbs are attractive to bees, so that a herb garden can be operated in conjunction with a beekeeping enterprise.

There are many excellent books on the cultivation and use of herbs. Among the best are *Elixirs of Life* by Mrs C. F. Leyel (Stuart and Watkins), *Herbs—How to Grow and Use Them* by Louise Evans Doole (Oak Tree Press), *Garden Herbs, Culture, Storage, Uses* by George E. Whitehead (A. & C. Black), *A Modern Herbal* by Mrs M. Grieve (Penguin), and *Herb Gardening* by Claire Loewenfeld (Faber and Faber).

Mushrooms

Outbuildings that are required for no particular purpose may be suitable for minimal conversion into mushroom houses, especially if there is a riding stable nearby from which it is possible to buy horse manure—the traditional and best medium for mushroom growing. The technique is not difficult to master and marketable crops are produced within a short time of starting. In late 1978, mushrooms were selling to wholesalers at 40 to 50p a pound.

At regular intervals the manure must be changed to prevent the build-up of disease. The exhausted mushroom compost can be applied to outdoor flower or vegetable beds.

Poultry

Raising chickens for the more obvious reasons—to supply the market with eggs and meat—does not rule out a traditional and specialist reason which is not connected with food at all. Less common breeds of chicken and bantam (a bantam is no more than a breed of chicken developed so that it remains small throughout its life, and bantams often mimic full-size breeds) are shown as a feature of all agricultural shows. At one time some of them were bred for fighting. Today they are bred purely for their attractive appearance. The birds and their eggs sell for high prices and there is a ready market for them among specialists.

Ducks are attractive creatures, not difficult to raise provided they can be protected against predators. It is easier to breed them if broody hens are available to hatch the eggs and raise the ducklings to a stage at which they can enter the water without becoming too chilled. Egg production is lower than with chickens and the market for duck eggs is limited. The adult birds can be sold for meat, but again the market is rather limited unless they are supplied fresh to restaurants or more specialist retail outlets.

Geese can be raised entirely on grass, so they are kept sometimes to help control grass in orchards and to keep away small boys. There is a rather limited demand for their meat, but those who like it find it preferable to turkey meat.

Like all young birds, goslings are very delicate during their first few weeks of life, but after that they are hardy, will find most of their own food, and need little attention. They require simple housing to provide shelter in bad, or hot sunny, weather. This may consist of a movable ark, shaped like a ridge tent with handles. (At 2m x 1½m, it will take five birds.) They will not eat long grass, which must be grazed down by other stock or mowed before the geese are turned on to it.

Turkeys can be raised profitably on a small scale for the Christmas trade, and there is no difficulty in selling them, because many people prefer fresh birds to frozen ones.

Breeding turkeys in the British climate is difficult and specialised. Most people buy poults in late summer, when they are about 6 weeks old and cost £2 or more each, depending on supply and demand. They must be protected until they grow the characteristic carbuncles on their throats, after which they are quite hardy. From then on they can be housed in pens or in a simple lean-to 'pole barn'. This is a wooden structure with the front covered with wire mesh. The floor should be covered with rubble or clinker to provide good drainage, and about 5 sq yd of space should be allowed for each bird. (A 2.5m x 1.2m house holds six birds of 17 weeks.) When young they eat a proprietary feed, which can be mixed with increasing amounts of moist bread or cake crumbs from the time they are 6 weeks old, giving way later to a

Movable housing for geese

Lean-to shelter for turkeys

diet of grain supplemented with greenstuffs.

Raising turkeys from poult to table weight is not difficult, but because of the way the industry works it is difficult to obtain poults except for fattening for the Christmas market.

Keeping Ducks, Geese and Turkeys by John Walters and Michael Parker, published in the Garden Farming Series by Pelham Books, provides a good introduction to the subject.

If you have, or can build, a dovecote, squabs (young birds) can be produced at practically no cost. A breeding population of pigeons is introduced and allowed to multiply until all the nesting sites provided have been occupied. After that, the squabs are sold for meat as soon as they are large enough. The birds are fed a certain amount of grain. If this is not sufficient they will steal the rest!

Rabbits

The rabbit used to be the animal raised in almost every back garden to provide a regular supply of cheap meat. As we became more prosperous we abandoned our old peasant ways and as war-time rationing ended, the rabbit fell from favour. Today it is becoming popular again, but most of the rabbit sold in British shops is imported from China.

The rabbit provides two products, meat and pelts. Depending on the degree of intensification, a doe will have 3 to 6 litters, producing 20 to 60 animals a year. The young will grow to a table weight of 2 to 3lb (liveweight of $4\frac{1}{2}$ to $5\frac{1}{2}$lb) in 9 to 14 weeks, again depending on the degree of intensification.

Each breeding doe, and the bucks, need one hutch per animal, but these can be arranged in blocks, one above the other, so that a number of hutches share a common roof and outside walls. Alternatively, they can be housed in a 'Morant', which is a movable house shaped like a ridge tent, solid and floored at the rear and constructed of a frame covered in wire mesh at the other. The floor of the open end must also be covered with mesh to prevent the does from burrowing. The house is moved over grass. It must be moved daily, but the rabbit finds much of its own food. If the hutches are permanent, food must be brought to the animals. The intensification of the system is based mainly on altering the diets of the rabbits from the greenstuff, acorns, bran, hay (in winter), bread and cooked potatoes supplemented by grain that is their usual fare, to one consisting mainly of grain prepared in pelleted form.

The Ministry of Agriculture, Fisheries and Food issues four Advisory Leaflets: *Rabbit Meat Production: General Management and Housing* (Leaflet 544); *Breeding Principles and Systems* (556); *Feeding of Meat Rabbits* (562); and *Breeds of Rabbits* (565). There are many books that provide an introduction to the subject, including *Rabbit Keeping* by C. F. Snow, which is one of the Foyles' Handbooks, and *Home Rabbit Keeping* by Marjorie E. P. Netherway, published as one of the Interest in Living Series by EP Publishing Ltd.

Reeds

The best material for thatching is *Phragmites communis*, the common or Norfolk reed. It is not confined to Norfolk, but will grow over most of Britain on the edges of still water or in very wet ground. Left to its own devices it will spread and form dense stands and it will cover the entire surface of shallow ponds as a stage in the ecological process whereby such ponds change to swamp, then marsh, and finally to dry land. The reeds have to be managed if such ponds are to be kept open. On the other hand, they can be allowed to occupy the entire area available to them and then cropped to provide a material for which thatchers will pay well. A reed-thatched roof will last 70 years or more before it needs renewing, compared with 10 or more years for one thatched with straw. What is more, modern varieties of wheat are short-strawed, so that good thatching material is more difficult to find than it used to be.

Rye

Very few farmers grow rye any longer. The total area devoted to it in Britain is about 15,000 acres. This sounds a lot until you remember that wheat occupies more than 2,500,000 acres and barley nearly six million. Rye is grown mainly to provide grazing for cattle. If it is sown in mid-summer, it may permit some grazing by November and this will stimulate good growth in spring, when it can be strip grazed, usually by dairy cattle, as soon as it is 8 to 10 inches tall. If it is not grazed, but allowed to grow to its full size, the crop can be even more useful. Its grain has a protein content equal to that of wheat and barley, but because it lacks the enzymes that produce gluten, it makes a heavy dough and dark, dense bread with a nutty flavour. This bread is popular among people who have acquired the taste for it and so there is a limited market for rye grain. It is also used in breakfast foods, so some can be sold for processing.

The more important crop, though, is the straw. Rye has not

been bred to dwarf varieties. It is 'unimproved' and grows to a height of 5 to 8 feet while yielding $2\frac{1}{2}$ times more straw than grain, by weight. The straw has almost no nutrient value to livestock, so it will not be eaten and can be used for bedding, especially for horses. It can also be used for thatching, for which it is by far the best of the straws.

A rye straw thatch will last 10 or more years. It is far less durable than reed, but land that grows reed will not grow rye, and vice versa. Rye prefers a light, sandy, slightly acid (about pH 5.5) soil that drains well. It must have a good texture and no plough pan. Cutlivation is minimal, consisting of little more than clearing the ground to prepare a seedbed. If farmyard manure is used to improve the soil structure, no additional fertilisers are required; if they are used, applications must be light (typically 0 : 75–150 : 75–150). Too much fertiliser, especially nitrogen, and this tall plant will grow still taller, produce an ear that is too heavy for the stem, and fall over in high winds or heavy rain. The process is called 'lodging' and it leads to heavy losses of grain and the ruination of the straw.

Silk

We associate silk production with Asia, but at one time Britain had a thriving silk industry and James I and VI, who encouraged it, is said to have planted so many mulberry trees that it is difficult to see how he managed to find time to do anything else.

The most usual silk worm, *Bombyx mori*, eats mulberry leaves and nothing but mulberry leaves. Other species of insect whose larvae produce usable silk are rather more versatile. For commercial production, though, *B. mori* is the animal you should use. Mulberry trees grow perfectly well in the British climate and the first step in silk farming is the establishment of a plantation of them, pruned so that they produce large crops of leaves but do not grow very tall. Once leaves are available the insects can be introduced. They must be housed indoors, in trays, at a little above normal room temperature, and fed fresh leaves. The extraction of the silk fibre from the cocoons is a skilled operation, but like all skilled operations it is one that can be learned. The feeding and rearing of silk moths is described in the *Silkmoth Rearer's Handbook*, obtainable from Worldwide Butterflies Ltd (see p. 189 for the address) which may be the only organisation seeking to revive silk production in Britain at present. They plan to market eggs as soon as they have sufficient.

Timber

Anyone who plants a tree that survives is, quite literally, a friend of the earth. In the world as a whole we are losing forest at such a rate that unless we slow down, all the great forests will have vanished within about 50 years. In Britain the great forests were felled to build the navy and to fuel the early stages of the Industrial Revolution, and in recent years Dutch elm disease has altered the landscape of much of the Midlands and southern England. We need many more trees than we have, and despite all the publicity and campaigning, new plantings are still insufficient to match losses from felling and disease.

Grants are available for tree planting. For small areas, up to half an acre, that will be improved aesthetically by planting, the Countryside Commission (see p. 187 for the address) can award grants worth up to 75 per cent of the cost of planting and caring for the trees until they are established. If the area is larger, from half an acre to 25 acres, the Forestry Commission (see p. 188 for the address) will give grants. Both organisations will provide advice and assistance both directly and in the form of leaflets.

For larger areas still, that will become useful managed woodland, the Forestry Commission will provide a great deal of help, much of it outlined in the booklet *Advice for Woodland Owners*, available free, from the Commission. There are various schemes that qualify for grants. If an area of woodland exceeding 25 acres is 'dedicated', the owner contracts with the Forestry Commission to manage it according to a plan worked out with its foresters to ensure good standards of forestry, effective integration with agriculture, environmental safeguards, and such public access as seems appropriate. In return, the owner receives a lump sum payment of

£40 an acre for coniferous woodland and £91 an acre for broad-leaved woodland, plus a further annual grant of £1.20 an acre for coniferous woodland less than 23 years old, and for broad-leaved woodland less than 50 years old. The higher lump sum grant is payable in Scotland for planting native conifers. Other grants are available for planting shelterbelts, since these are considered to enhance the agricultural or horticultural efficiency of the holding. The rate of grant varies from 10 to 30 per cent of the cost of planting and is 50 per cent of the cost for farms in less favoured areas.

Advice can also be obtained from The Woodland Trust (see p. 189 for the address) which is a voluntary organisation formed to purchase land for tree planting and to save forested land that is in danger of being lost.

Forestry is a long-term proposition, of course, and there is no way it can bring a quick return from investment. In the long term, though, it can be profitable, especially if the timber is sold not as standing timber but as finished wood products. If you are thinking ahead to a day 20 years from now when you hope to retire and live in the country, but you are able to buy a few acres of land now, a plantation laid down now will be ready to bring in a useful, and perpetual, income by the time you need it.

Tourism

Many farmers have discovered that caravans and tents are a more profitable crop than corn or cows. In fact, tourism now provides a large and important supplement to farm incomes in many parts of Britain.

To provide accommodation for a limited number of caravans and campers for a total of not more than 28 days in any one year, the farmer requires no planning permission; but if you wish to provide a site for a longer period you must have planning permission and you must provide adequate facilities. Lavatories, washrooms and refuse disposal bins are the minimum requirements, but most modern camp sites are expected to provide much more than this. The capital requirement could be high. The alternative is to provide more permanent accommodation in the form of chalets or flatlets for self-catering holidays and, if planning permission is obtained, these may qualify for capital grants.

Investment at this level is liable to turn the farm into a holiday camp that does little else. At a much more modest level, though, farmhouse accommodation is in great demand and provided the house in which you live is large enough to hold an additional family, the investment need not be great. You will need, obviously, additional linen, crockery and cutlery, and you may need additional cooking appliances and such machines as a dishwasher.

If you accommodate more than one family at a time, you may need to satisfy fire safety regulations; and your kitchen may have to be brought up to the standard of hygiene demanded of commercial catering establishments. It may sound slightly insulting, but catering standards are higher than those most of us accept in our own homes.

Tourism can be made profitable only in areas that are popular with tourists already, but the demand to spend holidays on working farms is such that it may be possible to offer farmhouse accommodation in what are presently unfashionable areas.

Vines

There are now more than 700 acres of commercial vineyards in Britain and viticulture is proving so popular that ADAS is conducting a proper costing of different methods to establish which are the most profitable.

Grape varieties have been developed that will produce wine-quality grapes in the open in the climate of southern England, and the yield can be impressive. One vineyard, in Somerset, occupies a 15-acre site and produces a total of 12,500 to 27,000 bottles of wine a year.

There are problems in Britain, due mainly to the climate. Ideally, vines need a total of 1,000 day-degrees to produce and ripen fruit. The 'day-degree' is a measure of the total warmth available during the growing season and it is used to estimate the probability of succeeding with species of plants that are close to the limit of their geographical range. In the hot summer of 1976, the only place in Britain to exceed 1,000 day-degrees was in Kent. If the site is good, it is possible to produce reasonable crops with as little as 800 day-degrees, but even this is difficult to achieve. Under glass, of course, vines can be grown very easily.

Grape varieties are divided into those that mature early and those that mature late, and only early varieties can be grown with even moderate confidence in Britain, the rule of thumb being that the further north you are the earlier the variety you need.

The site should be sloping to ensure good drainage, and facing south to provide maximum warmth. The soil should be poor. On rich soils vines develop luxuriant foliage but few grapes, and they are not encouraged to root deeply. As with all fruit growing, the trick is to remember that the fruit is the means by which the plant reproduces itself. If you threaten its survival by making conditions rather harsh, its response will be to reproduce in order to ensure the survival of its species. So the ideal soil is stony or gravelly, and very slightly alkaline (pH 7.0 to 8.0). In Britain, the site should not be too far above sea level. About 150ft is acceptable, but 300ft may be too high.

The production of wine from the grapes requires considerable skill, but this can be acquired. You must have a licence from HM Customs and Excise to make any fermented liquor on a commercial scale.

You can visit the Pilton Manor Vineyard in Somerset (see p. 189 for the address) and there are several books available describing the cultural methods used. A general introduction is given in *Home Farm* by Michael Allaby and Colin Tudge, published in hardback by Macmillan and in paperback by Sphere.

Willow

Land that is low lying and wet can usually be drained. This is expensive, however, and it is not always possible. An alternative may be to use it to grow willows to supply craftsmen engaged in basket work. Most of the willow used for basket making in Britain is grown in Somerset, and since willow is grown from cuttings you will need to obtain these from an existing grower. The Council for Small Industries in Rural Areas (CoSIRA, see p. 187 for the address) can supply the names and addresses of growers.

The growing of willows is not necessarily an easy option, for the land requires much cultivation before the sets can be planted. They used to say that it should be ploughed eight times. You will need 18,000 to 24,000 sets to the acre and they will produce their first full crop after three years. This should be 2 to 3 tons to the acre. Once established, the willow bed lasts for a very long time and 80 year old beds have been known.

Very basic instructions are given in *The Survival Handbook* by Michael Allaby, Marika Hanbury-Tenison, John Seymour and Hugh Sharman, published in hardback by Macmillan and in paperback by Pan.

The main outlet for the willow will be to makers of baskets and hurdles, but as with all primary produce, there are great advantages to be gained from processing it yourself as much as possible. Just as cheese sells for a higher price than milk, or fine linen than flax fibre, so finished basketwork is more valuable than the willow from which it is made.

9 Marketing

At one time many farmers suffered economically because, although they were perfectly well able to grow food, they had to sell it in a free, unregulated, and often local market. Today most of the major commodities are sold in more regulated markets, with guaranteed minimum prices, and to achieve this state of affairs it has been necessary to curtail some freedom of action of producers. The smallholder may feel the existence of state marketing boards is oppressive, but their effect has been beneficial. The monthly milk cheque paid by the Milk Marketing Board, for example, has ensured the well-being of the British dairy industry, and that embraces countless small family farms.

The MMB came under review by the EEC in 1978 because, under EEC law, no organisation can be permitted to exercise a monopoly control over any industry. Clearly, the MMB, and some other British marketing boards, are monopolies. The UK Government insisted that the MMB is popular among producers and that its operations were not felt to be restrictive. It was agreed, therefore, that before the law was implemented and the Board closed, a poll of dairy farmers, representing the vast majority of milk producers, should be held to assess its popularity among them. The Board would be permitted to continue if it could show that it had majority support. The result of the poll showed that more than 99 per cent of dairy farmers believed the Board should continue in its present form. The EEC doubts having been met, the MMB may remain in operation.

Commodities produced for a small, specialist market, must be sold by the producer; but for markets that involve state boards there are statutory requirements that the producer must meet. The marketing suggestions set out below, which include all the main produce boards and their requirements, are arranged alphabetically.

173

Apples and pears

If you have five or more acres of apple or pear trees, other than cider apples or perry pears, and you plan to sell the fruit, you must register with the Apple and Pear Development Council (see p. 187 for the address). The Council provides intelligence services, but does not impose any restrictions on producers.

Cereals

The Home Grown Cereals Authority (see p. 188 for the address) was formed by the Government in 1965 to promote more orderly marketing of home-grown cereals. It is financed partly by the Treasury and partly by a compulsory levy on all first sales of cereals. The levy is not paid by the producer, but by the dealer or processor, and it is used to provide a market intelligence service and to finance certain research and development.

Contract growing

The vegetables that are retailed deep frozen are grown under contract to the processing company. If your holding is within range of a processing factory (roughly 30 miles), then you may be able to grow crops under contract. Birds Eye Foods Ltd (see p. 187 for the address) are the largest company involved and they will provide you with detailed information about what they require. Essentially, the contract grower is guaranteed a price for his produce in return for certain guarantees regarding its quality. The processor provides the seed and advises on and supervises all the operations connected with its growth and harvesting. This includes instructions regarding the fertiliser to be used and the rate of application, and the disease, pest and weed control operations to be performed. Eventually, the crop will be harvested mechanically and farmers within a given area will be encouraged to form a syndicate to pool their labour. The aim, throughout, is to reduce production costs so that the two aims of a low price to the processor and a high price to the grower may be met.

The scheme sounds onerous, in that control of his growing is taken away from the grower who, in effect, rents his land and labour to the processor. This is true, but it is difficult to see how the industry could operate in any other way, since it must be able to guarantee a very high throughput for its processing plant. At the same time, standards of crop hygiene that are acceptable when vegetables are to be marketed fresh are not acceptable when the same crop is to be processed. A maggotty pea can be thrown away in the kitchen rather more easily than it can be identified, separated and removed in the factory, and a maggot that emerged from the frozen food package would be regarded as a more serious matter than one found in fresh produce.

If you live close to a cider or perry factory, you may be able to contract with the factory for the sale of your cider apples or perry pears.

Cooperatives

In Scandinavia the great bulk of farm produce is marketed by cooperatives formed and owned by the growers. In Britain the cooperative movement has been less popular. Some economists believe this is due to the association between the words 'cooperative' and 'socialist' in the minds of many ultra-conservative farmers. Be this as it may, there is no doubt that growers have much to gain from combining their forces. As the volume of produce increases, so does the bargaining power of the producer within his markets, and the increased bulk may generate sufficient additional income to pay for transport and administration. Marketing cooperatives may also develop into purchasing cooperatives, obtaining economies of scale on buying many commodities that individual members may need in insufficient amounts to qualify for bulk prices.

Producer cooperatives are encouraged by EEC regulations, and they may be eligible for grants under the Agricultural and Horticultural Cooperation Scheme, which is administered by the Central Council for Agricultural and Horticultural Cooperation (see p. 187 for the address), from which further information can be obtained.

Direct marketing

If your holding is too remote, or otherwise unsuitable for allowing access to the public, farmgate sales and 'pick your own' schemes are inappropriate. In such cases, it is possible to sell farm produce, of virtually any kind, directly to retailers without going through the wholesale system. It is a matter of private arrangement between the producer and each retailer or caterer, but usually it presents no difficulty beyond the expense of establishing a regular local delivery service. It is also likely to increase the price paid to the producer.

Eggs

If you produce eggs for hatching, or hatch your own eggs to provide replacement birds for your own flock, and if you sell eggs, you must register with the Eggs Authority (see p. 188 for the address), and pay a levy. You are permitted to recover the amount of the levy by adding it to the price of any chicks you sell.

Farmgate sales

In recent years there has been a rapid growth in sales of farm produce direct from the farm to the consumer, and this trend is likely to increase. There are very real advantages, since direct sales of this kind eliminate the whole of the marketing, retailing or processing systems. The consumer receives food that is fresher, the farmer establishes a direct personal relationship with those who eat the food he produces, and the economic saving is shared between producer and consumer, so that both benefit. Soft-fruit growers have found that by allowing the public to pick their own fruit, they have also saved on the most expensive item in soft-fruit growing, which is hand picking.

If you erect a permanent building as a shop, or convert an existing building to this use, you will need planning permission, and you must not erect a sign beside a main road without obtaining planning permission. On small roads you do not need permission for such a sign.

176

Obviously, your retailing operation must observe the principles of fair trading. You must give correct weights and measures, mark prices clearly, and not offend against the Trades Descriptions Act. The premises you use must conform to standards of hygiene appropriate to the produce being handled.

Hops

The Hops Marketing Board (see p. 188 for the address) has a monopoly on the marketing of hops grown in Britain, under the Hops Marketing Scheme 1932. If you wish to grow hops you must register with the Board, and if your application for registration is accepted you will be allotted an acreage for planting that you must not exceed.

Meat

The Fatstock Marketing Corporation is the largest meat trading organisation in Europe. It was established in 1953 as a farmers' cooperative intended to do for the marketing of meat what the Milk Marketing Board had done for milk. Over the years, however, it has become a large corporation virtually indistinguishable from other large corporations. It buys meat of all kinds on a deadweight basis, and it owns many abbatoirs and packing stations.

By paying a deadweight price, it differs from most other meat buyers, who make their purchases at regular auctions held in market towns, and who buy on a liveweight basis, guessing as best they can the actual amount of carcase meat on each animal.

The Meat and Livestock Commission (see p. 189 for the address) is a Government body responsible for administering the Fat Sheep Guarantee Scheme, the Calf Subsidy Scheme and the Beef Premium arrangements, as well as for various duties connected with the improvement of livestock breeds.

Cattle, sheep and pigs must be slaughtered at licensed abbatoirs according to humane methods laid down by law. You can slaughter small animals, such as rabbits or poultry, on your own premises. If these are for your own consumption or for sale direct to a local retailer or direct to a consumer, the premises need not be licensed. If they are for sale to a wholesaler, then your premises must be licensed for slaughter. In either case the law stipulates that animals must be killed by the most humane method. In the case of poultry this means by severance of the spinal column, either by breaking the neck or by decapitation.

If you take animals to be slaughtered and butchered elsewhere, it is not necessary for them to enter any kind of marketing system. You can have them back for your own use or for sale. To do this you must make a private arrangement with the abbatoir, pay a small charge for the service, and arrange delivery and collection. The abbatoir will kill, skin and joint the meat for you. You can then make other arrangements with processors, such as ham and bacon curers, to supply your own meat. You will pay for this service, collect your meat when processing is completed, and then you are free to use it yourself or to sell it.

Milk

If you plan to produce milk for sale, you must be registered as a dairy farmer under the terms of the Milk and Dairies (General) Regulations 1959. These Regulations lay down requirements for buildings and water supply which must be met before registration will be granted, and they stipulate methods of production which must be maintained. These are all summarised in a booklet, *A Guide to Clean Milk Production*, obtainable from Divisional Offices of the Ministry of Agriculture, Fisheries and Food, and it is to these offices that application for registration must be made. The addresses are listed in the telephone directory. As soon as you are registered by the Ministry you should contact the head office of the Milk Marketing Board (see p. 189 for the address). If you wish to sell milk other than to your own workers for their own consumption, you must register with the MMB.

If you wish to sell your milk wholesale, you must do so through the MMB. The Board will arrange with you to collect, either from your holding or from an agreed collection point. From July 1979, the use of churns will not be permitted by the MMB

178

anywhere in Britain. All milk will have to be stored in bulk containers while awaiting collection. The MMB will pay you a basic price for the milk (called the 'pool' price) from which it may make a deduction for transport costs. It will examine the quality of the milk regularly and if your milk does not meet MMB standards then a further deduction will be made from the price paid. Certain milk, such as Channel Islands milk, retails for a higher price and this is reflected in the price paid to the producer, which carries a premium added to the pool price. It may seem complicated, but providing the methods of production meet the standards laid down, the MMB tanker simply calls at the farm, collects the milk, and each month the Board sends you a cheque. As we saw earlier, the MMB also provides a great deal of advice and practical help to the dairy farmer, and it does not discriminate against the small, family farm.

In the rather unlikely event that the pool price falls below the CAP intervention price, and stays there for several months, the producer may withhold milk and sell it for processing into butter or skimmed milk, or sell it into intervention.

If you want to make cheese on the farm commercially, or if you wish to withhold some milk for any other reason, while still retaining a supply for wholesale sale, you can make an agreement with the MMB to withhold the amount you need.

You can also sell milk directly as a retailer, or bottle it on the farm for sale to a dairy. If you do this, or if you sell more than 50 gallons a year in connection with any catering establishment on your own farm, you must apply to the Ministry for a licence. You will be designated a 'producer–retailer' and the licence entitles you to opt out of the MMB marketing scheme. Under certain circumstances you can buy in milk from other farms to sell along with your own milk.

At present you can retail your own milk untreated, in which case it must be labelled 'unpasteurised'. Milk you buy in from other farms must be pasteurised before you sell it. The future of the retailing of unpasteurised milk is in the balance. It is official policy to end it, but when this was announced it provoked a strong protest from many producer–retailers, and the Ministry

179

hesitated while it reviewed the situation. In December 1978, the Ministry announced that the sale of untreated milk will be forbidden from 1 August 1983. Of course, pasteurisation is a sensible precaution, but opposition to it is based on nothing more subtle than the cost of installing pasteurising equipment. Farmers who cannot afford to do this may be forced out of their position as producer–retailers and may have to market through the MMB. There is a small market for unpasteurised milk among people who believe it has a higher nutritive value. So it has, but the differences are not nutritionally significant. Pasteurisation destroys about 20 per cent of the ascorbic acid, about 10 per cent of the thiamine and a smaller amount of the vitamin B_{12}, but milk is not an important dietary source for any of these vitamins. Old-fashioned sterilization caused greater losses, but its modern equivalent, Ultra High Temperature (UHT) treatment has an effect similar to that of pasteurisation, but increases the storage life of the milk considerably.

If you wish to pasteurise your milk on your own premises, you must apply for a licence to do so from the Ministry.

All milk sold directly to consumers, or to a dairy distributor, must be bottled or sealed in approved containers. It is illegal to sell loose milk off the farm.

None of these requirements or restrictions applies to goat's milk.

Organic foods

There is a small market for foods grown organically. At present the marketing arrangements for such foods relate mainly to fruit, vegetables and cereals, but in time they will extend to animal products as well. To qualify as an organic producer you must satisfy certain standards laid down by the voluntary organisations that supervise the system, principally the Henry Doubleday Research Association and the Soil Association (see p. 188 and 189 for their addresses). Market intelligence and the registration of producers is administered by Organic Farmers and Growers Ltd (see p. 189 for the address), which works rather like a producer cooperative and is financed by commission charged on produce sold through it.

Potatoes

If you wish to grow more than one acre of potatoes for sale, you must apply for registration with the Potato Marketing Board (see p. 189 for the address), which has a monopoly on potato marketing in Britain under the Potato Marketing Scheme 1955. The Board will allocate you an acreage for planting that must not be exceeded. Farmers who do plant more than their allotted acreage are fined. Registered potato growers must pay a levy to cover the operating costs of the Board, the size of the levy being related to the area planted, and part of the levy being refundable if the potatoes are lifted early in the season. You may sell potatoes for human consumption only to or through persons approved by the Board.

Sugar beet

You can grow sugar beet commercially in Britain only under contract to the British Sugar Corporation (see p. 187 for the address), which has a monopoly of sugar beet refining. Your application for registration will be approved only if the Corporation has a refinery in your area, and then you will be allotted an acreage to plant. The Corporation undertakes to pay the cost of transporting sugar beet to the factory and an allowance is made for the pulp content of the beet, both allowances being added to the basic price paid for the sugar content. Sugar beet pulp is used to make animal feedstuffs.

Wool

If you have more than four sheep, aged four months or more, and you wish to sell their wool, you must register with the British Wool Marketing Board (see p. 187 for the address). The Board has a monopoly of the marketing of wool in Britain under the British Wool Marketing Scheme 1950.

10 Whose countryside is it?

It pains me to have to say it, but farmers are regarded with some suspicion and hostility by conservationists, and for good reason. In general, they have a poor record when it comes to preserving areas of habitat for wildlife and a landscape that many people consider to be visually attractive. Nor do they welcome visitors on to their land.

It seems to me that there are two areas of disagreement. The first concerns what makes a landscape attractive, the second concerns the ownership of the land and the rights of the owner.

What is an attractive landscape? If you ask a town-dweller, you may be told that it is the kind of 'traditional' landscape, a landscape of small fields bounded by hedges and trees, what we might call a 'Constable' kind of landscape. If you ask a naturalist, you may be told that it is a rather wild, unkempt landscape, full of areas of comparative wilderness, in which wild plants and animals can live undisturbed. If you ask a farmer, however, you will be told that the most attractive landscape is the one in which no space is wasted, in which crops grow luxuriantly in fields free from weeds, a landscape that has hedges only where they are required to contain stock and where, for some reason, they cannot be replaced by cheaper and more efficient fencing. Trees, in this landscape, are confined to shelter belts and areas of woodland, and they are managed to produce a crop.

It is clear that three such divergent views can be reconciled only with the greatest difficulty. Yet some reconciliation is possible and little by little compromises are being made. People are learning that the 'traditional' landscape is, in fact, an Enclosure landscape, in many parts of Britain dating from the late eighteenth and nineteenth centuries, so that it is not really 'traditional' at all. The landscape of most of Britain has been manufactured by farmers as they have responded to the needs of their age. A wild, unkempt landscape may be one that does not produce food efficiently, and modern industrial societies need to produce food efficiently and in large amounts. At the same time, farmers are learning that although the landscapes depicted by Constable were produced by a form of agriculture that was not especially prosperous (look at the number of dilapidated vehicles and implements included in them) and that in modern terms is obsolete, these landscapes were aesthetically pleasing, and there is merit in the idea of preserving something of them. They are realising, too, that wildlife has a valid contribution to make to the quality of the countryside and that if it is to survive space must be allowed for it. In other words, the countryside has purposes other than those connected with the immediate production of food.

There are areas that have real scientific or scenic value. Their floristic composition may make them worthy of ecological study and, perhaps, preservation. In such cases they may be designated as nature reserves or Sites of Special Scientific Interest (SSSI). A nature reserve may be local or national and usually the land will be bought from the owner by the Nature Conservancy Council or by one of the voluntary organisations, such as the Royal Society for the Protection of Birds (RSPB) or a county naturalists' trust (the address of the county naturalists' trust is in the telephone directory; see p. 187 for the addresses of other organisations mentioned). If you think there may be such an area, extending at least to several acres, on your land, then you should contact one of these bodies, which will be glad to advise you. An SSSI is designated by the Nature Conservancy Council. The land does not change ownership and a designation on farmland may not necessarily require a modification of the farming pattern; but it does impose a planning constraint, making it more difficult to build on such land or to make fundamental changes. A site may contain archaeological material, or a building of historic interest, in which case it is possible to impose a form of protection on it. Usually, an arrangement is reached with the landowner either to preserve the site or to delay work on it until it has been excavated and anything of value recorded and, if necessary, removed.

These are comparatively rare cases, of course, although there are many SSSIs and archaeological sites located on private farmland. Even without such unique treasures, many farms have small areas that could be of value to wildlife. Odd corners, land that is low lying, wet and expensive to drain, and lengths of old hedgerow that link small areas of woodland, are all valuable as habitat, or potentially so. In many cases, no more is needed to improve them than to leave them alone for a few years. Where rather more sophisticated management is required, local naturalists' trusts will be glad to advise and they can also supply voluntary labour in many cases, through regional conservation corps. If you would like more information about the services to the countryside (but not to ordinary farming, where volunteers may turn into nothing more than cheap labour) offered by the conservation corps, you should write to their national organisation, the British Trust for Conservation Volunteers (see p. 187 for the address).

In some cases it is possible to obtain a grant to improve the habitat value of the countryside. You can find out more about this through the Farming and Wildlife Advisory Group, which you can contact through your county branch of the National Farmers' Union, whose address is in the telephone directory, from the RSPB, or from the Countryside Commission (see p. 187 for the address).

Areas of scenic beauty may be protected from undesirable developments by being designated Areas of Outstanding Natural Beauty (AONB), Heritage Coast, or, in the case of very large areas, National Parks. None of these designations is intended to impede farming, providing the farming does not drastically alter the character of the landscape that designation is intended to preserve.

Of these designations, only that of the National Park carries any requirement to improve public access to the land. Elsewhere, owners of suitable land may use this to provide Country Parks or picnic areas, for which they may be entitled to grants from the Countryside Commission.

Many farmers fear and resent attempts to improve public access to the countryside. Demand for such access has increased as the population has become more numerous, more prosperous, and more mobile, and it is likely to continue to increase even more.

Farmers claim that the land belongs to them and that the public has no more right to enter it than it has to enter private gardens. Where the public is permitted to enter, the Country Code promulgated by the Countryside Commission is not observed and damage is done. Gates are left open, fires are started, litter is left to cause injury to farm livestock, and animals are worried by dogs. Amenity groups, on the other hand, argue that the landscape of Britain is a part of our national heritage and therefore the property and legitimate concern of everyone. Thus no one has a right to prevent people from enjoying this heritage and ways should be found to facilitate such enjoyment.

As with most disputes, both sides are partly right and partly wrong. There is a confusion about ownership. Private individuals can own land, which is a physical entity, but they cannot own landscape, which is an abstract concept. However, the landscape derives its quality from the land and its management and so the enjoyment of landscape may require some constraint on the rights of owners. This idea is not new and the word 'ownership' means something subtly different when applied to land from what it means when applied, say, to a motor car. Land continues to exist in perpetuity, so that when it has ceased to be of use to one owner its ownership must pass to someone else. Thus, a concept of stewardship is inherent in the concept of the ownership of land. The landowner tends the land for a time before relinquishing it. It must be tended partly on behalf of the present owner, who derives immediate benefit from it, partly on behalf of those who will assume responsibility for it in the future, and partly on behalf of the community at large. If we accept that individual members of society are morally obliged to behave in ways that contribute to the continuance of that society, then the stewardship and, in a sense, the common ownership, of the natural resources of that society must follow. Of course, it can be argued that the individual has no obligation towards his fellows and no obligation to posterity. However, in practice we accept the former view. If a landowner were to sterilise his land deliberately, for example, say

185

by pouring a potent and persistent poison over it, we would regard this as a matter for legitimate public concern regardless of the fact that he might hold title deeds for the land. Similarly, if a landowner takes steps to enhance the fertility of the land, or its appearance or value, he receives public approbation. Such criteria are applied among farmers themselves.

This being so, the public has a right to take an interest in the welfare of agricultural land and it 'owns' the landscapes produced by agriculture. Indeed, this is a part of what we mean when we regard ourselves as citizens of a country for which we have a name. If there is a sense in which I 'belong' to England, then there is also a sense in which England 'belongs' to me.

Farmers, then, have no absolute right to exclude from their land anyone who seeks enjoyment of the countryside. Farmland cannot be compared to a private garden. By the same argument, the visitor to the countryside is obliged to behave in ways that do not damage the land or interfere with proper methods of husbandry. Unhappily, farmers do have good reason to fear the damage that can be caused by unthinking visitors. The solution, though, is not to exclude the visitors—which in any case is impossible—but to educate them.

There are, then, two sets of responsibilities, those of landowners and those of visitors to the countryside. It is natural, when considering ways in which a family may derive a living from working a small area of land, to concentrate on practical matters of husbandry and economic matters relating to produce and markets. Most farmers, most of the time, are obsessed with such considerations. Yet the countryside is more, much more, than a factory floor. It produces our food, timber and fibres, but the benefits it confers go much further than such material products, essential though they are. The countryside is the repository of much of what we consider to be beautiful, and it is the home of many non-human species that have a right to their own lives. Farmers of the future will make new landscapes as they made those of the past; but as they do they must find ways to accommodate wildlife in the new patterns and to allow people who are not members of the rural community to enjoy, appreciate, and learn to understand the beauty of those landscapes.

Useful addresses

Agricultural Credit Corporation, Agriculture House, 25–31 Knightsbridge, London SW1X 7NJ.

Agricultural, Horticultural and Forestry Industry Training Board, Bourne House, 32–34 Beckenham Road, Beckenham, Kent BR3 4PB.

Agricultural Mortgage Corporation, Bucklersbury House, 3 Queen Victoria Street, London EC4N 8DU.

AI Breeders' Services Ltd, 2a Banbury Road, Brackley, Northamptonshire.

Alfa-Laval Co Ltd, Farm Equipment Division, Oakfield, Cwmbran, Gwent NP4 3XE.

Apple and Pear Development Council, Union House, The Pantiles, Tunbridge Wells, Kent TN4 8HF.

Birds Eye Foods Ltd, Walton-on-Thames, Surrey.

British Bee-Keepers' Association, 55 Chipstead Lane, Riverhead, Sevenoaks, Kent TN13 2AJ.

British Goat Society, Lion House, Rougham, Bury St. Edmunds, Suffolk.

British Poultry Federation Ltd, High Holborn House, 52–54 High Holborn, London WC1V 6SX.

British Sugar Corporation, Central Offices, Oundle Road, Peterborough PE2 9QU.

British Trust for Conservation Volunteers, Zoological Gardens, Regents Park, London NW1.

British Wool Marketing Board, Oak Mills, Station Road, Clayton, Bradford, West Yorkshire BD14 6JD.

Bureau of Insemination Ltd, 9 Carlton Road, Burnley, Lancashire.

Central Council for Agricultural and Horticultural Cooperation, Market Towers, New Covent Garden Market, 1 Nine Elms Lane, London SW8.

Conservation Society, Food and Agriculture Working Party, 16 Conduit Road, Abingdon, Oxfordshire OX14 1DB.

Council for Small Industries in Rural Areas (CoSIRA), 35 Camp Road, Wimbledon Common, London SW19 4UP.

Countryside Commission, John Dower House, Crescent Place, Cheltenham, Gloucestershire GL50 3RA.

Crofters Commission, 4–6 Castle Wind, Inverness IV2 3EQ.

Cryoservice Ltd, 60 Hermiston Farm, Currie, Midlothian.

Cumbria College of Agriculture and Forestry, Newton Rigg, Penrith, Cumberland.

187

Department of Agriculture and Fisheries for Scotland, Chesser House, 500 Gorgie Road, Edinburgh EH11 3AW.

Eggs Authority, Union House, Eridge Road, Tunbridge Wells, Kent TN4 8HF.
English Vineyards Association, c/o Mrs J. G. Barrett, The Vineyards, Cricks Green, Felsted, Essex.

Field Stream and Covert (England) Ltd, Meriden, Warwickshire.
Forestry Commission, 231 Corstorphine Road, Edinburgh EH12 7AT.
R. J. Fullwood and Bland Ltd, Ellesmere, Shropshire SY12 9DG.

Glasshouse Crops Research Institute, Littlehampton, West Sussex.

Henry Doubleday Research Association, 20 Convent Lane, Bocking, Braintree, Essex.
Herring Industry Board, 1 Glenfinlas Street, Edinburgh 3.
Highlands and Islands Development Board, Bridge House, 27 Bank Street, Inverness IV1 1QR.
Home-Grown Cereals Authority, Hamlyn House, Highgate Hill, London N19 5PR.
Hops Marketing Board, 61 Maidstone Road, Paddock Wood, Tonbridge, Kent TN12 6BY.
Horticultural Education Association, College of Horticulture, Pershore, Worcestershire.
Horticultural Trades Association, Belmont House, 18 Westcote Road, Reading, Berkshire.

Institute of Park and Recreation Administration, Lower Basildon, Reading, Berkshire R98 9NE.
International Institute of Biological Husbandry, 62 Wilson Street, Finsbury Square, London EC2A 2BU.
International Institute for Environment and Development, 10 Percy Street, London W1P 0DR.
Intervention Board for Agricultural Produce:
    Steel House, Tothill Street, London SW1H 9LU.
    Fountain House, 2 West Mall, Butts Centre, Reading, Berkshire RG1 7QW.
    Government Buildings, Room GO3, St. Agnes Road, Gabalfa, Cardiff CF4 4YN.
    Chesser House, Room 513, 500 Gorgie Road, Edinburgh EH11 3AW.
    Dundonald House, Annex B, Upper Newtownards Road, Belfast BT4 3TS.

Kesteven Agricultural College, Caythorpe, Grantham, Lincolnshire.

Land Settlement Association, 43 Cromwell Road, London SW7 2EE.

Meat and Livestock Commission, Queensway House, Bletchley, Milton Keynes MK2 2EF.

Micron Sprayers Ltd, Three Mills, Bromyard, Herefordshire HR7 4HU.

Milk Marketing Board, Thames Ditton, Surrey KT7 0EL.

Ministry of Agriculture, Fisheries and Food (Publications), Tolcarne Drive, Pinner, Midllesex HA5 2DT.

Ministry of Agriculture, Fisheries and Food, Directorate of Fisheries Research, Fisheries Laboratory, Lowestoft, Suffolk NR33 0HT.

National College of Agricultural Engineering, Silsoe, Bedfordshire MK45 4DT.

National Farmers' Union, Agriculture House, Knightsbridge, London SW1X 7NJ.

National Institute of Poultry Husbandry, Harper Adams Agricultural College, Edgmond, Newport, Salop TF10 8JB.

Natural Energy Association, 161 Clarence Street, Kingston-upon-Thames, Surrey KT1 1QT.

Nature Conservancy Council, 19 Belgrave Square, London SW1X 8PY.

Organic Farmers and Growers Ltd, Longridge, Creeting Road, Stowmarket, Suffolk IP14 5BT.

Pilton Manor Vineyard, Pilton, Shepton Mallet, Somerset.

Plumpton Agricultural College, Plumpton, Lewes, Sussex BN7 3AG.

Potato Marketing Board, 50 Hans Crescent, London SW1X 0NB.

Rare Breeds Survival Trust, 127 Abbots Road, Abbots Langley, Hertfordshire WD5 0BJ.

Royal Horticultural Society, Vincent Square, London SW1.

Royal Society for the Protection of Birds, The Lodge, Sandy, Bedfordshire.

Scottish Agricultural Society, 48 Palmerston Place, Edinburgh 12.

Soil Association, Walnut Tree Manor, Haughley, Stowmarket, Suffolk IP14 3RS.

University of Reading, Department of Agriculture, Earley Gate, Reading, Berkshire.

Usk College of Agriculture, Usk, Gwent NP5 1XJ.

West of Scotland Agricultural College, Auchincruive, Ayr, Scotland KA6 5HW.

White Fish Authority, Sea Fisheries House, 10 Young Street, Edinburgh EH2 4JQ.

Women's Farm and Garden Association, Courtauld House, Byng Place, London WC1.

The Woodland Trust, Butterbrook, Harford, Ivybridge, Devon.

Worlds Poultry Science Association (UK) Ltd, BOCM Silcock Development Farm, Risborough Road, Stoke Mandeville, Aylesbury, Buckinghamshire.

Worldwide Butterflies Ltd, Sherborne, Dorset DT9 4QN.

Index

192